THE WAY
PEOPLE
LIVE

Life in Ancient Rome

THE WAY
PEOPLE
LIVE

Life in Ancient Rome

by Don Nardo

Lucent Books, P.O. Box 289011, San Diego, CA 92198-9011

Library of Congress Cataloging-in-Publication Data

Nardo, Don, 1947–
    Life in ancient Rome / by Don Nardo.
        p.   cm. — (The way people live)
    Includes bibliographical references and index.
    Summary: Describes the customs and day-to-day life of the inhabitants
of ancient Rome.
    ISBN 1-56006-335-1 (alk. paper)
    1. Rome—Civilization—Juvenile literature.   2. Rome—Social life
and customs—Juvenile literature. 3. Rome—Civilization.
[1. Rome—Social life and customs.] I. Title.   II. Series.
    DG78.N355   1997
    937—dc20   96-14184
                                                                                    CIP
                                                                                    AC

Contents

Discovering the Humanity in Us All

The Way People Live series focuses on pockets of human culture. Some of these are current cultures, like the Eskimos of the Arctic; others no longer exist, such as the Jewish ghetto in Warsaw during World War II. What many of these cultural pockets share, however, is the fact that they have been viewed before, but not completely understood.

To really understand any culture, it is necessary to strip the mind of the common notions we hold about groups of people. These stereotypes are the archenemies of learning. It does not even matter whether the stereotypes are positive or negative; they are confining and tight. Removing them is a challenge that's not easily met, as anyone who has ever tried it will admit. Ideas that do not fit into the templates we create are unwelcome visitors—ones we would prefer remain quietly in a corner or forgotten room.

The cowboy of the Old West is a good example of such confining roles. The cowboy was courageous, yet soft-spoken. His time (it is always a he, in our template) was spent alternatively saving a rancher's daughter from certain death on a runaway stagecoach, or shooting it out with rustlers. At times, of course, he was likely to get a little crazy in town after a trail drive, but for the most part, he was the epitome of inner strength. It is disconcerting to find out that the cowboy is human, even a bit childish. Can it really be true that cowboys would line up to help the cook on the trail drive grind coffee, just hoping he would give them a little stick of pep-

permint candy that came with the coffee shipment? The idea of tough cowboys vying with one another to help "Coosie" (as they called their cooks) for a bit of candy seems silly and out of place.

So is the vision of Eskimos playing video games and watching MTV, living in prefab housing in the Arctic. It just does not fit with what "Eskimo" means. We are far more comfortable with snow igloos and whale blubber, harpoons and kayaks.

Although the cultures dealt with in Lucent's The Way People Live series are often historically and socially well known, the emphasis is on the personal aspects of life. Groups of people, while unquestionably affected by their politics and their governmental structures, are more than those institutions. How do people in a particular time and place educate their children? What do they eat? And how do they build their houses? What kinds of work do they do? What kinds of games do they enjoy? The answers to these questions bring these cultures to life. People's lives are revealed in the particulars and only by knowing the particulars can we understand these cultures' will to survive and their moments of weakness and greatness.

This is not to say that understanding politics does not help to understand a culture. There is no question that the Warsaw ghetto, for example, was a culture that was brought about by the politics and social ideas of Adolf Hitler and the Third Reich. But the Jews who were crowded together in the ghetto cannot be understood by the Reich's politics. Their life was a day-to-day battle for existence, and the creativity and methods they used to prolong their lives is a vital story of human perseverance that would be denied by focusing only on the institutions of Hitler's Germany. Knowing that children as young as five or six outwitted Nazi guards on a daily basis, that Jewish policemen helped the Germans control the ghetto, that children attended secret schools in the ghetto and even earned diplomas—these are the things that reveal the fabric of life, that can inspire, intrigue, and amaze.

Books in the The Way People Live series allow both the casual reader and the student to see humans as victims, heroes, and onlookers. And although humans act in ways that can fill us with feelings of sorrow and revulsion, it is important to remember that "hero," "predator," and "victim" are dangerous terms. Heaping undue pity or praise on people reduces them to objects, and strips them of their humanity.

Seeing the Jews of Warsaw only as victims is to deny their humanity. Seeing them only as they appear in surviving photos, staring at the camera with infinite sadness, is limiting, both to them and to those who want to understand them. To an object of pity, the only appropriate response becomes "Those poor creatures!" and that reduces both the quality of their struggle and the depth of their despair. No one is served by such two-dimensional views of people and their cultures.

With this in mind, the The Way People Live series strives to flesh out the traditional, two-dimensional views of people in various cultures and historical circumstances. Using a wide variety of primary quotations—the words not only of the politicians and government leaders, but of the real people whose lives are being examined—each book in the series attempts to show an honest and complete picture of a culture removed from our own by time or space.

By examining cultures in this way, the reader will notice not only the glaring differences from his or her own culture, but also will be struck by the similarities. For indeed, people share common needs—warmth, good company, stability, and affirmation from others. Ultimately, seeing how people really live, or have lived can only enrich our understanding of ourselves.

Rome's Blueprint for Success

"Even as I speak I see our destiny," wrote the Roman poet Ovid, "the city of our sons and sons of sons, greater than any city we have known, or has been known or shall be known to men."[1] Ovid lived and wrote in the final years of the first century B.C., when the Romans controlled an empire stretching from the Atlantic coast of Spain in the west to the deserts of Palestine in the east, a vast realm in the midst of which the Mediterranean Sea was, in a very real sense, a Roman lake. Like most of his countrymen, he was proud of Rome, its many accomplishments, and its civilization, which by his day had already thrived for nearly eight centuries. In fact, pride in the past, enhanced by a conservative attitude that aimed to perpetuate the ways of that past, was a major facet of the Roman character. "This thing, Rome, is simply men who know what their past means,"[2] commented the second-century Roman writer Quintus Ennius. Their conservative attitude had a profound effect on the Romans' everyday lives, for they routinely looked to the past for inspiration on how to live in the present.

Other facets of the Roman character also contributed to shaping the Romans' daily lives. First, they were an unusually hardy, stubborn, and determined people. Time after time during their long history they suffered crises and crippling hardships and seemed on the brink of total ruin, yet refused to admit defeat and eventually emerged stronger than ever. For example, in the Second Punic War,

fought against the powerful mercantile city-state of Carthage in the third century B.C., the Romans experienced their worst battlefield defeat ever (more than fifty thousand

The toga, in ancient times an article of clothing traditional to and distinctly characteristic of Roman citizens.

In the climax of the Third Punic War, the Romans besiege Carthage, the prosperous and powerful city-state that had once controlled the western Mediterranean. After killing or enslaving the inhabitants, the Romans mercilessly destroyed nearly every building and plowed the site with salt.

killed in a few hours) and then went on in succeeding years to lose almost an entire generation of Roman men. Yet in the span of little more than a decade they rallied heroically and delivered Carthage a crushing defeat, from which it was never fully able to recover.

The Romans showed the same grim and gritty determination in almost everything they did. Faced with the threat of a huge and formidable enemy navy in their first war with Carthage, and having no warships or naval tradition of their own, they proceeded to build some 140 fully equipped warships in only sixty days, a phenomenal accomplishment. The second-century B.C. Greek-Roman historian Polybius remarked that this feat "shows us better than anything else how spirited and daring the Romans are when they are determined to do a thing."[8]

Secondly, the Romans were a highly practical people, in large degree because their ambitions and conquests forced them to be so. "Roman genius was called into action by the enormous practical needs of a world empire," famed classical scholar Edith Hamilton has written.

> Rome met [these needs] magnificently. Buildings tremendous . . . where eighty thousand could watch a spectacle, baths where three thousand could bathe at the same time . . . along with them the mighty Roman road . . . marching on and on irresistibly . . . to the very edges of the habitable world. This is the true art of Rome . . . its keen realization of the adaptation of practical means to practical ends, its tremendous energy and audacity and pride.[4]

This pragmatism extended into every aspect of Roman life, from the art of building to the art of war. It even helped to shape the way people worshiped. "Roman religion was quite shockingly practical," scholar Harold Mattingly points out in *The Man in the Roman Street*.

> It was concerned essentially with things as they are and did not venture after difficult and unaccustomed moralities. It implied a practical explanation of the world as we know it and practical precepts [rules] as to how to gain its prizes and escape its perils. It demanded from the plain man no great intellectual effort and no uncommon goodness.[5]

Part of the Romans' practical genius was their talent for imitating others, their ability to recognize the best attributes of foreign cultures and to adapt these to their own special needs. The first-century B.C. Roman politician-historian Gaius Sallustius Crispis, popularly known as Sallust, described his

This carving on the side of a well-to-do Roman's sarcophagus depicts part of a triumphal procession, probably to celebrate a military victory.

A reconstruction of the magnificent Forum Romanum, Rome's main square, as it appeared in the first century A.D.

ancestors' talent: "Whatever they found suitable among allies or foes, they put in practice at home with the greatest enthusiasm, preferring to imitate rather than envy the successful."[6] For example, the *scutum*, the characteristic rectangular shield that helped propel Roman soldiers to victory after victory, was adapted from the Samnites, an Italian tribe they conquered and absorbed in the late 300s B.C.

More than anyone else, the Romans imitated the Greeks. An energetic, artistic, and brilliantly creative people, the Greeks, especially the Athenians, developed an advanced culture, including magnificent art, architecture, and literature, in the fifth and fourth centuries B.C. In the following two centuries, the Romans, culturally crude by comparison, conquered first the Greek cities of southern Italy and eventually the Greek city-states and kingdoms of the eastern Mediterranean. The Romans were immediately captivated by many Greek ideas and accomplishments. But their urge to borrow and adapt what they admired conflicted with another of their characteristic traits, their belief that their way of life was superior and that their destiny, ordained by the gods, was to rule others. According to noted historian Michael Grant:

> The Romans' attitudes to the Greeks posed a historic dilemma. On the one hand, they were well aware that the Greeks were their cultural superiors, and indeed, that it was to the Greeks that they themselves owed their own entire culture. On the other hand, they felt [great] contempt and dislike for contemporary Greeks.[7]

The great first-century B.C. Roman orator Marcus Tullius Cicero, for instance, praised the Greeks for their "knowledge of many arts," for "the charm of their speech," and for "the keenness of their intellects." But he went on to point out that a Greek could not be trusted because "he does not think of the worth of his oath."[8] Thus, Cicero held, the Greeks, while talented, were, like all other peoples, inherently morally inferior to Romans.

This superior attitude, reflected so unabashedly in Ovid's references to Rome's destiny and greatness, motivated the Romans to conquer and rule nation after nation. Such vaunting conceit combined with dogged determination, practical genius, and other facets of the Roman character to produce what amounted to a blueprint for success. For some twelve centuries, these stalwart traits constituted the foundation on which the Romans fashioned their everyday lives and built one of the greatest civilizations in history.

CHAPTER 1

Rungs on the Social Ladder: The People of the Roman State

Rome, the so-called Eternal City that was the political and cultural hub of the ancient Mediterranean world for nearly seven centuries, is located at a bend in the Tiber River about 15 miles from Italy's western coast. Italy itself, composed mainly of a 600-mile-long and roughly 150-mile-wide peninsula, the famous "boot," juts down into the blue waters of the Mediterranean and, along with the large island of Sicily at the "toe" of the boot, divides the sea into its western and eastern spheres. Thus, geographically ancient Rome occupied an opportune central position allowing easy access to the lands and peoples along the sea's thousands of miles of coastline.

The early Romans were Latins, one of a group of primitive nomadic tribes that migrated from central Europe southward over the Alps and into Italy between 2000 and 1000 B.C. By the latter date, the Latins had settled the fertile plain they came to call Latium, nestled between the western seacoast and the rugged Apennines, which run north-south through the Italian boot. And by about 750 B.C. the largest villages in the region had combined to form a crude farming community known as Rome. The name supposedly came from the legendary figure Romulus, who, the later Romans believed, founded the city in 753 B.C. and served as its first king.

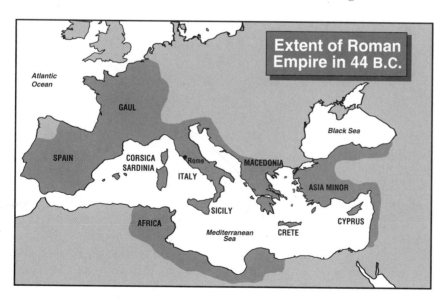

Extent of Roman Empire in 44 B.C.

Atlantic Ocean
GAUL
Black Sea
SPAIN
CORSICA SARDINIA
Rome
MACEDONIA
ITALY
ASIA MINOR
AFRICA
SICILY
CYPRUS
Mediterranean Sea
CRETE

In the Ranks of Roman Society

The fact that Rome evolved from an ancient tribal society, one based principally on the ownership and exploitation of land, profoundly influenced the development of its family and social structure and the status, both public and private, of that structure's various members. Before and during the dimly remembered era of Romulus, the chief landholders emerged as the wealthiest and strongest figures in the community. Each of these *patres*, or fathers, who united politically to form the state, headed a separate *gens* (plural, *gentes*), a tribal clan made up of several extended families related by blood.

The clan heads constituted the early Roman nobility. From their title of *patres* came the term *patrician*, describing the wealthy and privileged class they composed. Their influence, stemming from their *dignitas*, or prestige, and their *auctoritas*, or moral authority, extended not only over the many members of their individual gentes, but also over the state. The strongest of their number became king and the others served as *senatores*, members of an advisory council called the Senate. According to historian R. H. Barrow:

> Apparently, a new king was appointed by the heads of the leading families . . . and the choice was confirmed by the community as a whole. The king held supreme power (*imperium*), appointed officials, dispensed justice, led in war, and ordered religious worship. The Senate was the council of the heads of the leading families; they were members for life.[9]

Later, about 509 B.C., the senators dispensed with the kingship and established an oligarchy (from a Greek word meaning "rule of

A fanciful depiction of Romulus, Rome's legendary founder and first king, wearing a laurel wreath, a symbol of honor and glory.

the few"), in which the Senate itself largely governed the state. This marked the beginning of the Roman Republic, usually dated from 509 to 27 B.C., the first of Rome's two major historical periods. The second was the Roman Empire, lasting from 27 B.C. to A.D. 476, in which the Senate was again subordinate to a single ruler, this time an emperor.

Throughout most of these centuries, the landowning patricians remained Rome's most privileged, respected, and envied social class and the most politically powerful of the Roman *cives*, or citizens. During the Republic, as Rome's expanding empire became powerful and prosperous, a few businessmen gained great wealth and prominence and formed a non-land-based aristocracy second in prestige only to the patricians. This was the equestrian class. As Michael Grant explains, these two groups, representing only a tiny fraction of the population, managed to control society partly because Roman law

was biased in favor of the privileged classes, and . . . their words and persons carried an ill-defined but very real authority [*auctoritas*], based on the social estimation of their honor and the prestige [of] their position. . . . The ruling groups controlled . . . and exploited the labor which . . . they needed in order to enforce their power. . . . It was wealth that gave honor to Rome. Landed wealth was the only truly respectable asset—and the best thing of all was to have inherited it.[10]

The labor that the upper classes exploited consisted partly of slaves but also comprised the lowest and poorest class of citizens, the plebeians, or plebs, who made up the bulk of the population. The privileged classes controlled the plebs in another way through the patronage system, in which the heads of well-to-do families became the *patroni*, or patrons, of less well-off *clientes*, or clients. A patrician patron's dependent plebeian clients voted as he directed and supported him in other ways in exchange for his financial and legal protection. "The very root of Roman society," Grant adds, "was the institution of a relatively few rich patrons . . . linked with their more numerous poor clients."[11]

Not all clients were poor, however, for the patronage system extended throughout the ranks of Roman society. Though a well-to-do aristocrat had many clients of his own, he, in turn, was client to someone even more wealthy or powerful. The most obvious example was during the Empire, when Rome's elite sought and benefited from the emperor's patronage.

The Family and Its Head

Supporting the clans, the class structure, the patronage system, and the rest of the framework of Roman society was its most basic and time-honored unit—the family. That the Latin word for family, *familia*, translates literally as "household" is revealing. In contrast to the small nuclear families (consisting of a mother, father, and their children) common today, most Roman families were extended, typically including father and mother; unmarried daughters; sons and adopted sons, either married or unmarried, and their wives, sons, and unmarried daughters; and any uncles, aunts, and cousins who, for one reason or another, had no one to support them.

This bust of an unknown man from the first century A.D. captures typical Roman character traits—hardy practicality, austerity, and a touch of arrogance.

The head of the family was the paterfamilias (plural, patresfamilias), usually the oldest father present. By ancient tradition, he held power and authority known as *patria potestas* over all other members of the household, including, of course, any slaves or hired workers who lived with the family. Scholar Walton B. McDaniel writes:

> The absolute power that the head of the house could exercise over his dependents not only gave him the complete disposal [control] of all property that they might earn or acquire, but even permitted him to decide whether a new-born baby should be deprived of life or reared, whether a penalty for disobedience should be some mild punishment or . . . banishment or death.[12]

At least these were the powers that early custom and law allowed the paterfamilias. In actual practice, most family heads were not merciless tyrants. Cases of fathers throwing out their wives or children or killing them were relatively rare and occurred mostly in Rome's earlier centuries. Over time, new laws set certain restrictions on the *patria potestas*, and in any case calls from a father's relatives, friends, and peers for him to act reasonably tended to restrain him from excessively cruel behavior. According to scholar Harold W. Johnston, "Custom, not law, obliged the paterfamilias to call a council of relatives and friends when he contemplated inflicting severe punishment upon his children, and public opinion obliged him to abide by its verdict."[13]

A notable exception was the practice of exposure—leaving an unwanted infant outside to die, usually in some deserted spot. Roman families, at the direction of their patresfamilias, regularly exposed deformed or severely handicapped babies, and some

A Grim Toll of Dead Children

Infant mortality, the death rate of babies and young children, was a factor that profoundly affected the size and character of Roman families. Excluding the purposeful practice of exposure, factors such as poor sanitation, disease, and high rates of miscarriage and death during childbirth took a grim toll, so that few Roman couples had more than two or three children who lived to adulthood. Examples abound. Tiberius Gracchus and his wife Cornelia, parents of two famous second-century B.C. social reformers, had twelve children, only three of whom survived. Julius Caesar's only daughter, Julia, died while giving birth to her only child, who died at the same time.

The emperors Tiberius and Domitian each had only one child, both of whom died in infancy. After losing all five of his children one after another, the noted second-century A.D. orator Marcus Cornelius Fronto wrote in his *Correspondence*, "I never had a child born to me except when bereaved of [mourning] another." Even when children managed to survive infancy and early childhood, many died in their teens or as young adults due to war, disease, and other factors. To his frustration and sadness, Augustus Caesar, the first Roman emperor, long outlived his nephew, son-in-law, stepson, and two grandchildren.

evidence suggests that more than a few infant girls, less prized than boys in a society so highly male dominated, met the same fate.[14] Not all such abandoned babies died, however. A fairly large proportion were rescued by childless couples or by people seeking an easy profit. Classical scholar J. P. V. D. Balsdon writes, "The infant could by law be brought up either as a free child or as a slave, in which latter case he or she could be sold or exploited when adult, showing a handsome profit over and above the expense of upbringing."[15] In the third century A.D. the practice of exposure declined as increasing numbers of Romans came to look upon it as murder, and it was finally outlawed in 374.

The Changing Lot of Roman Women

Traditionally, the materfamilias, the paterfamilias's wife or mother, was also subject to the absolute authority of the male head of household. Though Roman women were considered citizens, like women in other ancient societies they did not enjoy the same rights as male citizens. In the early years of the Republic, Roman men treated women largely as inferiors, mainly because men saw themselves as more intelligent and competent. As Cicero, writing in the more enlightened and less chauvinistic first century B.C., explained: "Our ancestors established the rule that all women, because of their weakness of intellect, should be under the power of guardians."[16] These guardians were always men, who controlled the property of their wives, mothers, and daughters, and barred them from voting, holding public office, or initiating divorce proceedings.

By Cicero's time, the lot of Roman women had improved considerably and it

The features portrayed in this bust of an unknown first-century A.D. Roman matron express confidence, dignity, and an air of serenity.

continued to improve in the first two centuries of the Empire. Women gained the rights to inherit and control their own property, to file for divorce at will, and in most (though certainly not all) households became more men's partners than their servants. The high degree of love and respect many men came to feel for their wives is illustrated by a letter the first-century A.D. writer Pliny the Younger penned to his wife while she was away:

> To Calpurnia: It is incredible how I miss you; such is the tenderness of my affection for you, and so unaccustomed are we to a separation! I lie awake the greatest part of the night in conjuring up your image, and by day . . . my feet carry me of their own accord to your apartment, at those hours I used to visit you; but not finding you there, I return with as much sorrow and disappointment as an excluded lover.[17]

Unlike Greek women, who spent most of their hours locked away in the "women's quarters" of their homes and rarely socialized with men, Roman women regularly attended parties and public functions with their husbands and enjoyed a degree of freedom unprecedented in the ancient world. According to Johnston:

> No other people held its women in such high respect; nowhere else did women exert so strong . . . an influence. In her own house the Roman matron . . . directed its economy and supervised the tasks of the household slaves, but did no menial work herself. . . . She was her husband's helpmate in business as well as in household matters, and he often consulted her on affairs of state.[18]

A few women even ventured into roles and occupations usually filled only by men. Cases of female doctors, writers, business owners, and even gladiators have been documented. It should be noted, however, that despite many rights and freedoms gained during the famously liberal Roman Empire, Roman women never acquired the rights to vote or hold public office; and the duration and breadth of their educations never equaled those of men.

Foreigners, Slaves, and Freedmen

Women were not the only people in the Roman world who were denied equal rights with male *cives*. Foreigners, called *peregrini*, were allowed to do business with Roman citizens but not allowed such basic rights of citizenship as voting and serving in the army. The *peregrini*, whose ranks for a long time included provincials, the residents of Rome's many provinces, also had to pay various taxes from which citizens were exempt. Over time, the status of provincials improved markedly. For example, laws evolved providing that if a provincial married a citizen the former automatically received full citizens' rights. Finally,

This carved stone relief depicts settlers in a Roman-occupied Germanic province paying taxes to a local magistrate in the third century A.D.

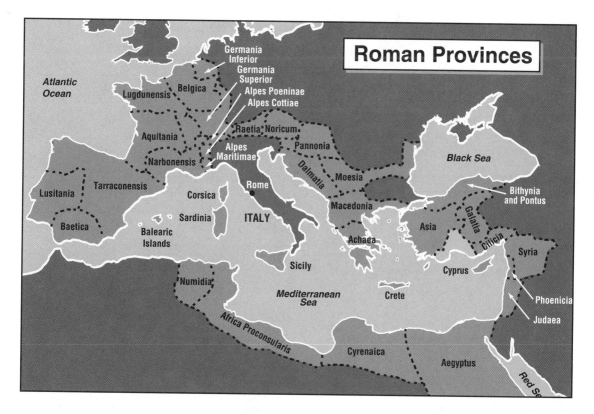

Roman Provinces

in A.D. 212 the emperor Caracalla extended full citizenship to all free provincials and from that time on the term *peregrini* referred only to residents of nations outside Roman-controlled territory.

Slaves, of course, never enjoyed the civil rights of free Romans. During the Republic, most slaves were prisoners captured in war. During the Empire, when Rome waged few foreign wars, owners replenished their slave ranks by encouraging their slaves to couple and have children or by buying new ones in foreign slave markets. Accurate data concerning the number of slaves in the average household or in society in general have not survived. Apparently about 5 to 10 was the minimum for an equestrian or patrician of moderate means, but richer individuals owned 60, 70, or even hundreds of slaves. The famous Roman writer and naturalist

Pliny the Elder mentioned one owner, Gaius Caelius Isidorus, who owned 4,116 slaves! [19] Most historians estimate that in the early years of the Empire slaves made up from one-quarter to one-third of the total population of Italy.

Slavery was a wretched and inhumane institution no matter where or when it existed. Yet it was an accepted fact of life everywhere in the ancient world, condoned and practiced even by freedmen, or former slaves (the notorious slave owner Isidorus mentioned by Pliny was himself a freedman); and it is noteworthy that the Romans, principally during the Empire, made considerable strides toward making slavery more humane. As scholar Leonardo B. Dal Maso points out in *Rome of the Caesars*, the lot of Roman slaves "was considerably less unhappy and inhumane than it was among other peoples

Slaves are displayed and inspected on an auction block in a Roman slave market. Like all other ancient peoples, the Romans viewed slavery as a natural, acceptable, and necessary fact of life.

both in ancient times and in the medieval and modern periods. Proof of this are the severe laws which protected them and determined their treatment."[20] These laws included, among many others, an edict in the first century A.D. by the emperor Nero (urged on by his adviser, the writer Seneca, an advocate of humane treatment for slaves) allowing slaves to register complaints of unjust treatment by their masters; a law passed in A.D. 83 under the emperor Domitian forbidding a master from castrating his male slaves; and finally, under the emperor Antoninus Pius in the second century, a law branding as a murderer any master who killed his slave.

Indeed, many slaves became important, outspoken, trusted, and even loved members of Roman households. Many Roman tombstones and surviving writings contain warm and sincere tributes to deceased slaves, among them this example by the first-century A.D. poet and humorist Martial: "To you, my parents, I send on this little girl Erotion, the slave I loved, that by your side her ghost need not be terrified of the pitch darkness underground."[21]

Many slaves, particularly those who worked in households, received periodic gifts of money or even small but regular wages from their masters, enabling some to save enough eventually to buy their freedom. Other slaves became freedmen when a kind owner freed them as a gesture of thanks for years of loyal service. About Roman freedmen, scholar Paul Veyne comments:

Freed slaves usually did not live in the home of their former master, although they continued to come there [as clients] to pay him homage. Set up in business as artisans, shopkeepers, or merchants, they accounted for less than 5 percent of the total population; yet they formed a group that was highly visible socially and very important economically. Although not all shopkeepers were freed slaves, all freed slaves were shopkeepers and traders.[22]

Thus, freedmen contributed to the growing ranks of the middle class, especially during the early centuries of the Empire.

What's in a Name?

A discussion of the different kinds of Roman people would be incomplete without considering the names these people used. Roman names had much more profound meaning and importance than those in modern societies because they denoted social status and family history as well as personal identity. For example, a free Roman male used his nomen, the name of his clan, which often indicated social rank and status. Nomina ending in the suffix *-ius* (or variations like *-eius* or *-aius*), such as Fabius, Julius, and Cornelius, were ancient clan names reserved for patricians.

Less prestigious nomina had endings such as *-acus*, *-enus*, and *-ca*.

Roman men also used two other names—the cognomen, denoting the particular extended family within the specified clan, and the praenomen, or first name, identifying the individual himself. The normal order of the three names was praenomen, nomen, cognomen. Thus, the famous politician-general Gaius Julius Caesar could be identified as Gaius of the family of Caesar of the clan of Julius. To the frequent frustration of modern historians and students, the normal order of these names was often changed for various reasons, such as in the case of poets

The Woes of Luckless Poverty

The bitter feelings of many poor plebs toward wealthy upper-class patricians and equestrians were captured by the poet and humorist Decimus Junius Juvenalis, popularly known as Juvenal, who lived from about A.D. *60 to 130. In his famous* Satires, *critical but often witty observations of Roman life, he wrote:*

"The hardest thing to bear in poverty is the fact that it makes men [appear and feel] ridiculous. 'Out of those front row seats,' we're told [by the marshal at the theater or arena]. 'You ought to be ashamed of yourselves—your incomes are far too small, and the law's the law. . . . Let your place be occupied by [higher-class people].' . . . What prospective son-in-law ever passed muster here if he was short of cash to match the girl's dowry? What poor man ever inherits a legacy [worthy inheritance], or is granted the meanest of appointments—a job with the Office of [Public] Works? All lower-income citizens should have marched out of town, in a body, years ago. Nobody finds it easy to get to the top if meager resources cripple his talent. But in Rome the problem's worse than anywhere else. Inflation hits the rental of your miserable apartment. . . . Your humble dinner suffers inflation too. You feel ashamed to eat off of earthenware dishes. . . . To cut a long story short, nothing's for free in Rome."

Juvenal, whose surviving satires offer priceless and fascinating insights into ancient Rome's customs and class system.

trying to match the names to rhymes or meter.

Adding to the complexity and confusion was the frequency of legal adoption in Rome and the name change that went with it. "When a man passed from one family to another by adoption," Johnston explains, "he regularly took the three names of his adoptive father and added his own nomen modified by the suffix -anus."[23] Thus, when the young man born Gaius Octavius Caepias (who would later become Augustus, the first Roman emperor) was adopted by Gaius Julius Caesar, he became Gaius Julius Caesar Octavianus. Still another name, an honorary title called the *cognomen ex virtute*, was often awarded to great statesmen or victorious generals. In this way, after Lucius Aemilius Paulus was adopted by Publius Cornelius Scipio and then distinguished himself as a military commander in Africa, he became known as Publius Cornelius Scipio Aemilianus Africanus!

Women's names were much less complex, at first. In the Republic, most young girls went by a feminine form of the father's nomen, so that Gaius Julius Caesar's daughter was called Julia and Marcus Tullius Cicero's daughter was known as Tullia. Later, however, in the Empire, when women's status had increased, writes Johnston, "we find the threefold name for women in general use, with the same riotous confusion in selection and arrangement as prevailed in the . . . names of men at the same time."[24]

The names of slaves and freedmen, except in the early days of the Republic, were no simpler. At first, slaves were called *por*, a slang version of the Latin word *puer*, meaning "boy," and identified with their master's praenomen. Thus, Marcipor was "Marcus's boy," Aulipor was "Aulus's boy," and so forth.

This relief decorating a tomb from republican times shows a likeness of the man buried inside, flanked by portraits of his trusted freed slaves.

The Emperor's Many Slaves

In the Roman world, not even the wealthiest patricians could compete with their emperors in the sheer numbers of slaves owned and exploited. Some emperors had as many as twenty thousand slaves to complete the huge number of tasks that went into supporting the imperial household. A typical emperor owned so many material things and lived on such a grand scale that his slaves became extremely specialized, each usually performing one specific task all of his or her life. For example, slaves who made and maintained the emperor's palace clothes were called *a veste privata*; his city clothes, *a veste forensi*; his full-dress parade uniforms, *a veste triumphali*; and his theater clothes, *a veste gladiatoria*. Some slaves did nothing but polish his eating utensils, while others polished only his drinking cups. Those who bathed him were called *balneatores*; those who massaged him, *aliptae*; those who cut his hair, *tonsores*; and those who later dressed his hair, *ornatores*. Among the many other types of slaves the emperor employed were jewel keepers, pearl keepers, at least four kinds of butlers, several kinds of cooks and bakers, furnace stokers, waiters who only served food, waiters who only removed dirty dishes, food-tasters, musicians, and dancing girls. With so many dutiful attendants, it is no wonder that many Roman emperors led lives of unprecedented luxury and leisure.

Later, however, slaves were given a personal name, usually of foreign origin, as well as the nomen and praenomen of their masters. More confusing yet were freedmen's names, which consisted of their original slave name, followed by the nomen of the former master, then by a cognomen assigned at will by the master when freeing the person, and finally by the letter *L*, which stood for *libertus*, the Latin word for freedman. In response to Shakespeare's famous question "What's in a name?" Romans of all walks of life, always conscious of and sensitive about family affiliations and the status of their particular rung on the social ladder, would undoubtedly have answered, "A great deal!"

CHAPTER 2

The Mind and Heart of the State: Roman Government and Law

Excluding the early and relatively brief kingship, two distinct Roman states governed Rome and the lands it controlled during its long history: the Republic and the Empire. These political entities were superficially very different. The Republic was a representative form of government, guided by officials elected by the people, at least in theory. By contrast, the Empire operated largely according to the whims of a single man, the emperor, whose word was law; again, at least in theory.

In truth, beneath the surface the structure of the Roman state did not change all that much as the Republic fell and gave way to the Empire. The Senate and many other republican institutions remained in place throughout the years of the Empire, and although they lost much of their earlier authority they, along with the Roman legal system, were the foundation on which the emperors based their own authority. This was because the Romans were deeply connected to their past and desired to maintain continuity with it. The symbol of the Republic displayed on documents and monuments—SPQR, which stood for *Senatus Populusque Romanus*, "the Senate and People of Rome"—continued as the official mark of the Empire. As Harold Mattingly puts it, the motto of both Republic and Empire "might be taken to be 'as things have been they remain.' . . . The slogans that represent the general attitude toward the future are not 'progress' or 'reform,' but . . . 'eternity, perpetuity, restoration of the times of happiness.' "[25]

Thus the emperor, though very powerful, could not seriously abuse his authority, for to do so meant going against centuries of cherished tradition as well as a huge body of

Early Roman consuls and senators, charged with carrying out state foreign policy, listen to greetings by an envoy from another land.

accepted laws, which Cicero called the "mind and heart of the state." The few emperors who did lapse into tyranny, notorious characters like Caligula, Nero, Domitian, and Commodus, provoked public outrage and met violent ends. Though the years of the Empire were in many ways more liberal, both socially and legally, than those of the Republic, the Roman people remained basically conservative and traditional. After many centuries of accepted precedent, they expected, and when necessary demanded, fair treatment under the majestic protective umbrella of Roman law.

The Branches of Government

However, the idea that all citizens, regardless of wealth or social position, should receive fair treatment under the same set of laws was not exactly what the *senatores* had in mind when they threw out their king and established the Republic in 509 B.C. Such democratic concepts developed over the course of centuries as Roman law itself grew and expanded to meet changing human needs. The rich and aristocratic patricians who founded the Republic were primarily concerned with maintaining their authority and, not surprisingly, fashioned the government, clearly an oligarchy, to serve their own interests.

The Roman fathers divided the state into two branches, one administrative, the other legislative. The administrative branch consisted of two top officials, called consuls, initially always patricians, who served jointly for one year. According to classical historian Chester G. Starr, the consuls

supervised the government at home and acted as generals abroad. Although in the field each consul usually operated independently with his own army, in Rome both had to concur [agree] if any serious political action was to be taken. In critical emergencies the consuls stepped aside to make way for a single dictator with overriding powers, who was appointed for 6 months.[26]

Thus, when Carthage's Hannibal invaded Italy and directly threatened Rome in the Second Punic War, the serving consuls were temporarily replaced by a trusted citizen named Fabius Maximus, who fortified the city and for six months orchestrated all state policies and war strategies. A dictator's term was both short and nonrenewable in order to keep any single individual from amassing too much power.[27]

Supporting the consuls were other administrators. These included eight praetors, who managed the legal system and also administered the city when both consuls were absent; eight (and later as many as twenty) quaestors, in charge of financial matters such as taxation and paying the army; four aediles, who supervised public buildings, markets, and roads, and also organized public games and entertainments; and nine pontiffs, religious officials who, under the guidance of the chief pontiff, the *pontifex maximus*, supervised public religious sacrifices and festivals.

The Roman founding fathers ordained that most of these officials be elected. But, in keeping with their elitist political outlook, they made sure that the candidates and most voters were members of the upper classes by limiting citizenship, voting, and office-holding rights to free adult males who owned weapons, which at the time were very expensive. These privileged citizens met periodically in the Centuriate Assembly to discuss important issues, formulate new laws, and elect public officials.

In time, most and then all of the more numerous plebs qualified for citizenship. They objected to being left out of the political process and, through mass protests, won the right to their own legislature, the Popular, or Tribal, Assembly. They then began annually electing ten unique public officials called

tribunes to defend their interests. Starr writes:

> Initially the tribunes protected their fellow plebeians in matters of taxes and the draft [call-up for military service], but eventually they claimed and won the right to say "Veto!" (I forbid) against any unjust action of the government within

Duties of the Censors

Although not as publicly visible as the consuls, praetors, and aediles, another group of Roman officials, the *censores*, or censors, performed crucially important duties. Two new censors were elected every five years from a pool of former consuls. In this excerpt from his *On the Laws*, Cicero described most of the main duties that went with this office.

> Censors shall list all citizens [that is, conduct a public census], recording their age, antecedents, families, and means. They shall supervise the city's temples, roads, [and] water system [by awarding contracts for their construc-

tion and upkeep]. . . . They shall divide citizens into tribes and list them also according to wealth, age, and [social] rank. They shall assign young men to the cavalry and infantry. They shall discourage the unmarried state, guard public morality, and suspend from the Senate anyone guilty of improper conduct.

About every eighteen months, after completing their assigned duties for that period, the censors conducted a great religious ceremony in which they prayed to the gods to increase the prosperity of the Roman state and its people.

Censors and their scribes (at far left) conduct a periodic census of the populace.

the city of Rome. . . . A tribune was considered sacrosanct [secure from assault], that is, anyone interfering with a tribune or injuring him was made an outlaw.[28]

The tribunician power became an effective way for lower-class Romans to check and balance the occasional abuses of authority by the upper-class consuls and senators.

"The Best People" Versus "the Mob"

At first glance, having two assemblies in which citizens suggested laws and voted to elect leaders might seem quite democratic. However, the real power in Rome rested in the third and most important legislative body, the Senate. The senators, on average numbering about three hundred, were all aristocrats, as well as former consuls and other high officials, and they served for life. They reserved the rights to control public finances, to decide most foreign policy, and to administer the provinces. Even more importantly, they advised the consuls, usually determining major policies, and, utilizing the patronage system, used their influence to sway the way citizens voted in the assemblies. "A senator was not a man like other men," Paul Veyne explains. "Whatever he said was public and was supposed to be believed." Also, through the moral authority of his *auctoritas*, which was "naturally" his, he "was entitled to say how any citizen worthy of the name ought to live."[29]

The traditional power of the oligarchic Senate was what kept Rome from evolving into a true democracy. This is not surprising, considering that the senators were part of the ancient and venerable patrician elite. They doubted the intelligence, abilities, and moral

A view from one wing of the Senate House, where the Roman fathers debated and decided on weighty affairs of state.

capacity of the common people, whom they often referred to as "the mob." Cicero, for instance, was a great champion of republican government over tyranny, yet as a senator and an aristocrat he strongly believed that a little democracy was good, but too much was dangerous. Arguing that society's "best" people ought to govern the others, he wrote: "The possession and use of political power shall be in the hands of men of goodwill [that is, upper-class men] . . . so that liberty may consist in the very fact that the people are given an opportunity of honorably gaining the favor [through patronage] of those men."[30] He argued further that according equal honor and authority to society's highest and lowest would be unfair to both. The highest were by nature superior, he reasoned, and therefore deserved to rule, while the lowest would be

The great politician and orator Marcus Tullius Cicero, last important champion of the dying Republic, delivers a speech in the Forum Romanum.

incapable of ruling well even if given the chance. However, Cicero stated, "this cannot happen in states ruled by their best citizens."[31]

Princes with Responsibilities

Cicero, in fact, turned out to be the Republic's last important champion. In the late first century B.C., after a series of ruinous civil wars in which powerful military generals vied for control of the state, Julius Caesar's adopted son Octavianus, popularly known as Octavian, emerged triumphant. Having outmaneuvered and defeated the last credible republican forces, Octavian established a

new political structure—the Empire—on the wreckage of the Republic, with himself firmly in charge. But he did so quite cleverly and skillfully, avoiding the image of a grasping tyrant or military dictator. He wisely allowed the Roman people their all-important continuity with their past by keeping the Senate, the consuls, and other republican institutions in place and ruling in their name. The Senate, therefore, willingly conferred on him the title of Augustus, "the most revered and exalted one." And when it became apparent that he was a peace-loving, fair, and constructive leader, the people gladly named him "father of his country."

The political philosophy Augustus left to the line of emperors who followed him was not all that different from that practiced by Cicero and his senatorial colleagues. Both systems acknowledged that society's "best"

A posthumous and idealized bust of Augustus Caesar, who preferred the title princeps, *or first citizen, to that of emperor.*

Democracy Unworkable?

After the fall of the Republic, Octavian, soon to become Augustus Caesar, the first Roman emperor, wrestled with the problem of how to structure Rome's new government. Like the aristocrats who preceded him in the Republic, he rejected the concept of democracy as unworkable, supposedly after hearing the advice of his close associate Gaius Maecenas. According to the second-century A.D. historian Dio Cassius in his Roman History, *Maecenas declared that democratic institutions would be too weak and undisciplined to administer an empire as large as Rome's.*

"The cause is the immense size of our population and the magnitude of the issues at stake. Our population embraces every variety of mankind in terms both of race and character; hence both their tempers and their desires are infinitely diverse, and these evils have gone so far that they can only be controlled with great difficulty. Our past bears witness to the truth of what I have just said. So long as our numbers were not large and we did not differ in any important respects from our neighbors, our system of government worked well, and we brought almost the whole of Italy under our rule. But ever since we ventured beyond our native soil, crossed the water, set foot on many islands and many continents, and filled the whole sea and the whole earth with our name and power, we have experienced nothing but ill-fortune."

people should lead due to their inherent superiority. The people were willing to accept that superiority as fact as long as an emperor lived up to his own responsibilities as the *optimus princeps*, or best possible citizen, from which the term "best of princes" developed. These responsibilities, Mattingly writes, were to be "pious in the service of the gods, just in his dealings with his subjects, strong and victorious in the face of the enemy, but merciful after victory; he must be temperate and kind, and . . . love peace and concord, those precious gifts without which states collapse into decay."[32]

Not all of the Roman emperors lived up to this virtuous ideal. But some did, most notably those who ruled in the second century A.D., when the Empire enjoyed its greatest size and prosperity during the second half of the *Pax Romana*, or "Great Roman Peace," which began with Augustus. In any case, it usually mattered little to average Romans whether they were ruled by good or bad emperors, or even by good or bad senators and consuls. Throughout most of Roman history, the common masses had little real say in government. The concept that concerned them most and that most affected their everyday lives was that of receiving fair treatment under the law, no matter who was in charge.

A Civilization Upheld by Law

The great body of Roman law was the main structural link between the Republic and Empire, preserving the best of the political and legal tradition of Rome's past, while continually growing and adapting to the needs and demands of changing times. Writes Edith Hamilton:

Rome's monumental achievement was law. A people violent by nature . . . produced the great Law of Nations which sustained with equal justice the rights of free-born men everywhere. . . . Along with the tremendous Roman roads and aqueducts went the ideal of which they were the symbol, civilization founded and upheld by law.[33]

"Of all sets of laws ever compiled," Michael Grant adds, "theirs comes nearest to universal acceptability."[34]

Above all, Roman law was based on common sense and practical ideas. What seemed obvious to the Romans (and still does to us) was that written laws should reflect naturally existing principles of justice that apply to all citizens within a state. "Those who share law, share justice also," wrote Cicero in his *De Legibus (The Laws)*. "Moreover, those who share law and justice ought to be considered to belong to the same state, all the more so if they obey the commands of the same authorities." Cicero also equated law with logical

and practical wisdom, or reason, saying, "The prime link between man and God is reason. . . . And since law is reason, we ought to think that law also links man with the Gods."[35]

The first application of these and other rational legal concepts occurred in about 450 B.C., when the Romans wrote down their first set of laws in the so-called Twelve Tables. This famous code, like many other laws that followed, emphasized individual citizens' rights, especially rights pertaining to the ownership of property. For instance, one law protected the individual by allowing him to sue for injury: "If he [the attacker] has broken or bruised [a] freeman's bone with hand or club, he shall undergo [a] penalty of 300 pieces [of gold or silver]." A landownership law stated: "Should a tree on a neighbor's farm be bent crooked by the wind and lean over your farm, you may . . . take legal action for the removal of that tree."[36] Later laws, which were developed and altered as social conditions warranted, dealt with inheritance, women's rights, money matters, masters ver-

Augustus (seated at left with scroll) reads to a group of citizens in the Forum. His highly productive forty-five-year reign, characterized by peace, prosperity, artistic expression, and massive building programs, later became known as the Age of Augustus.

Roman citizens inspect and discuss carved copies of the Twelve Tables, Rome's first written law code.

a trial. If it was, they chose a *judex*, or judge, to hear the case (or, on occasion, heard it themselves), after which the plaintiff, the individual bringing the case to court, summoned the defendant, the person being sued or accused of wrongdoing.

The trial, called the *judicium*, took place in a basilica, a large building also used for public meetings and usually located near the forum, a city's main square. Generally, in the more routine cases plaintiffs pleaded their own cases and defendants defended themselves. However, in a more serious case a litigant often hired a professional lawyer, called an *advocatus*, who, if he frequently won, was highly respected and in demand.[37] The juries who heard such cases were composed of as many as seventy-five *judices*, or jurors (all of them citizens), to make tampering with or bribing a jury impractical if not impossible.

Punishments following a guilty verdict depended partly on the defendant's social status and partly on the severity of the offenses. Wealthy and prominent individuals rarely received the death penalty; and, because of their high standing in the patronage system, they often got off with lighter sentences than did poor plebs. The penalties for minor crimes, such as fraud or not fulfilling a contract, usually consisted of paying a fine or compensating the victim. Even those convicted of serious crimes usually did not go to prison. Instead, they received sentences ranging from exile to distant parts of the empire, to loss of citizenship and property, to execution by crucifixion, beheading, or having to fight another criminal to the death in the arena.

Roman government, law, and justice were no more nor less perfect than their modern counterparts. But the Roman system, in which fair and durable laws protected all citizens, rich and poor, and in which an

sus slaves, and many other issues, even moral behavior. But all, right down to the Empire's final years, continued to use the laws in the Twelve Tables as precedents.

Crime and Punishment

Practical application of the law was the task of the extensive and largely fair Roman court system. The praetors, who managed the courts, decided whether a case was worthy of

The Foundation of Liberty

In his oration *Pro Cluentio* (quoted by Michael Grant in *The World of Rome*), Cicero, perhaps Rome's greatest law advocate, pointed out that personal liberty in any state could not exist without a fair code of laws.

> Law is the bond which secures these our privileges in the commonwealth [empire], the foundation of our . . . liberty, the fountainhead [main source] of justice. Within the law are reposed the mind and heart, the judgment and the conviction of the state. The state without law would be like a human body without mind—unable to employ the parts which are to it as sinews [tendons], blood and limbs. The magistrates [officials] who administer the law, the jurors who interpret it—all of us in short—obey the law to the end that we may be free.

Cicero did not mean "free" in the liberal democratic sense, as embodied in the U.S. Bill of Rights with its long list of personal freedoms. Rather, he meant freedom in the collective sense, the freedom of a people, in this case the Romans, from a tyrannical system in which the law changed according to the whims of a despotic ruler. Indeed, even in the autocratic Roman Empire, with very rare exceptions, the strong and unchanging buttress of accumulated laws provided an umbrella of protection for Romans of all classes.

accused person was considered innocent until proven guilty, was unique in the ancient world. In the mid–second century A.D., at the height of the magnificent *Pax Romana*, the Greek orator Aelius Aristides summed up in his *Roman Panegyric* the genuine admiration that so many people of the age felt for that successful system:

> You [Romans] who hold so vast an empire and rule it with such a firm hand . . . have very decidedly won a great success, which is completely your own. . . . There is an abundant and beautiful equality of the humble with the great and of . . . the commoner with the noble. . . . Your ways and institutions . . . are ever held in honor and have become ever more firmly established. . . . Let all the gods . . . grant that this empire and its city flourish forever . . . and that the great governor [the emperor, at the time Antoninus Pius] and his sons be preserved and obtain blessings for all. [38]

CHAPTER 3

Two Worlds Intertwined: Country Life Versus City Life

The various aspects of Roman life, like those of the Greeks and other ancient peoples, were for the most part divided into two major spheres: the rural countryside and the urban city. Though physically very different, country and city were to a large extent dependent on each other. In order to feed their large populations, cities had to import food from farms in the countryside, and the fortunes of most of the rich city-dwellers, including nearly all of the patricians, were based on the ownership and exploitation of farmlands. "Agriculture was the Empire's major industry upon which all else depended," scholar Joan Liversidge points out, "and the purchase of land was considered to be the safest and the one really reputable form of investment."[39] In turn, many farmers depended for their livelihoods on the markets in nearby cities and towns, where they sold their crops and livestock.

The importance of farming and country life in the Roman world cannot be overstressed. It is a common misconception that the contrast between rural and city life then was similar to that in modern developed countries like the United States, where most people live in cities and suburbs and import food from a handful of rural farmers. By contrast, in the Roman Mediterranean the vast majority of people lived in the countryside and grew their own food. Large cities were rare. In the early Empire, Rome had a popu-

lation of about a million; Alexandria, Egypt, about six hundred thousand; and Antioch, in the province of Syria, and Roman Carthage, in the province of Africa, each perhaps a few hundred thousand. Outside of these, most so-called cities were, by modern standards, just small towns. For example, the now-famous Pompeii (buried by a volcanic eruption in A.D. 79 and excavated largely intact in modern

In this reconstruction of a street scene in ancient Pompeii, patrons stop at a local snack bar (rear) for a late-afternoon meal.

"A Really Fine Property"

This excerpt from a late first-century A.D. letter by Pliny the Younger (from his *Letters*, Book III, 19), seeking advice from his friend Calvisius Rufus about expanding one of his country estates, illustrates how important investing in and exploiting land was to Roman men of means.

> An estate is offered to be sold which [borders] mine. . . . There are several circumstances which strongly incline me to this purchase. . . . The first recommendation it has is, that throwing both estates into one will make a really fine property; the next, the advantage as well as the pleasure of being able to visit it . . . to have it looked after by the same agent, and . . . to have only one villa [country manor] to maintain hand-

somely. . . . I believe I may get it for three millions of *sesterces*.

Pliny's lands were small compared to the large farming enterprises known as *latifundia* that grew numerous in Italy during the second and first centuries B.C. and drove increasing numbers of small farms out of business. In his work *On Agriculture*, composed about 160 B.C., the rich senator and landholder Marcus Cato advocated that large farming estates could make the best profits from growing vines for making wine and olives for producing olive oil. He also advised using slave labor because it was cheap and offered many other tips on how a Roman gentleman could exploit his own "really fine property."

---

times), which was a typical Roman town, had no more than twenty thousand inhabitants. Accurate population figures for most Roman regions have not survived but evidence suggests that in some areas country dwellers outnumbered city dwellers by factors of four, eight, or even more.[40]

Nevertheless, cities were vital centers of commerce, culture, and learning, and, for those who could afford them, were filled with comforts and conveniences usually lacking in the country. The Roman upper classes, Paul Veyne writes,

> were a nobility of the cities, who visited their rural estates only during the heat of the summer. . . . A city was not so much a place of familiar streets and bustling anonymous crowds as an array of material conveniences such as public baths and buildings, which lifted the spirits of resi-

dents and travelers alike and made the city much more than just a place where numbers of people lived.[41]

Thus, the contrasting worlds of the Roman city and countryside existed side by side, economically intertwined and interdependent, both with unique and essential facets of life.

The Harsh Realities of Farm Life

Because Rome had originally begun as a farming society and because agriculture remained the main basis of its economy, urban and rural Romans alike had a strong emotional attachment to country life. According to scholar Garry Wills, "Romans always had a sharp nostalgia for the fields. Even their worst poets surpass themselves when a landscape is to be described. And all of them associated morality with simplicity, simplicity with the countryside. The city was foul, the country pure."[42] One of Rome's best poets, the first-century B.C. writer Publius Vergilius Maro, popularly known as Virgil, extolled the perceived virtues of pastoral life in many of his works. In the *Eclogues*, first published in 37 B.C., he described the joy of an elderly man lucky enough to call a piece of the lovely and restful countryside his own:

Happy old man! So these lands will still be yours, and large enough for you [in your old age]. . . . Here, amid familiar streams and sacred springs, you shall court the cooling shade. . . . The hedge whose willow blossoms are sipped by . . . bees shall often with its gentle hum [of breezes blowing through it] soothe you to slumber. . . . Under the towering rock, the woodsman's song shall fill the air.[43]

No doubt the Italian countryside in Virgil's time was at least as beautiful as it is today. However, such idealized and idyllic views of the fields were largely those of the members of upper classes who did not have

A Roman peasant carries his produce to market. Farmers were most often poor and had to work long hours to eke out meager livings.

to work in them. The harsher reality was that the vast majority of rural people were poor farmers, whose lives consisted mainly of long days that became years of backbreaking toil for which material rewards were few and meager.

With the help of his wife, children, and sometimes a slave or hired hand if he could afford it, the average farmer grew grains, such as emmer wheat, to make flour for bread, a staple food. Autumn was planting season. Using an *aratrum*, a crude ox-drawn wooden plow sometimes equipped with an iron blade, one person broke up the earth, while a second tossed the seeds by hand from a bag hung around the neck. Harvest time was April or May, when the workers cut the grain using a *falx*, a sickle with a curved blade and handle, a Roman invention. After collecting the crop, they threshed it, or separated the grain from the stalks, by having horses trample it on a stone floor. Usually, a farmer sold whatever his family did not eat to a *pistor* (plural, *pistores*), a combination miller and baker who crushed the grain using a millstone called a *meta*, fashioned it into dough, and then baked it in an oven heated by charcoal.

Grains were not the only output of small farms. They also grew vegetables and fruits, including carrots, radishes, cabbage, beans, beets, lentils, peas, onions, grapes, plums, pears, and apricots. These and other crops grew well in Italy and several of Rome's provinces, which benefited from the pleasant Mediterranean climate, consisting of short, mild winters followed by long, hot, and sunny springs and summers. "Italy is blessed above all the other countries of central Europe," Harold Johnston writes, "with the natural conditions that go to yield an abundant and varied supply of food. The soil is rich . . . the rainfall is abundant, and rivers

and smaller streams are numerous."[44] The climate and soil were particularly favorable for growing olives, a crop second in importance only to wheat. Some olives were eaten. Most, however, were pressed to produce olive oil, which the Romans and other peoples used in cooking, as a body lotion and perfume ingredient, and as fuel for oil lamps. Farmers also raised livestock, including goats, chicken, geese, ducks, sheep, and pigs. They slaughtered some animals to eat themselves and sold the surplus.

In the first few centuries of the Republic, many such small farmers owned their own land, a typical holding consisting of two to five acres at most. But over time increasing numbers found it impossible to compete with huge farming estates, called *latifundia* (singular, *latifundium*), covering hundreds or even thousands of acres. Owned by rich absentee landlords who lived in splendid houses in the cities, and utilizing the cheap labor of many slaves, these estates cornered the agricultural market by the early years of the Empire. They owed part of their success to special deals cut with the *censores*, who leased them large portions of *ager publicus*, lands taken by Roman conquest, at low cost. Some of the poor farmers driven out of business by the big estates migrated to Rome and other cities in search of work. Many others became *coloni*, tenant farmers who worked small portions of the *latifundia* in exchange for a share of the harvest.

Features of a Typical City

The system in which rich city dwellers exploited the countryside emphasized the economic connection between the urban and rural spheres. As Paul Veyne points out, Roman cities "were essentially places where

Merchants display their wares to crowds of shoppers in an outdoor marketplace in Rome's colonnaded main forum.

Roman notables . . . spent the money generated by land. The Roman Empire thus stands in sharp contrast to the France of the Middle Ages, where the nobility lived scattered about the countryside in fortified castles."[45] Indeed, despite their frequently professed yearning for the idyllic countryside, most well-to-do Romans preferred the densely packed, fast-paced city, which featured the services and conveniences needed to support their lifestyle of leisure and *luxus*, or luxury.

That most Roman cities were designed for function and convenience is apparent in their layout. Typical small cities like Pompeii were built on a rectangular grid pattern, with two main roads meeting at right angles in the center, where the chief public buildings were situated. The main square, or forum, used as a marketplace and for public meetings, was an open area surrounded by shops and offices, usually with colonnades, column-lined roofed walkways, in front of them. According to Liversidge:

The inhabitants met in the forum to shop and exchange news. In bad weather the colonnades provided shelter, and advertisements or election notices were often scribbled on the columns. Across [one] end of the forum was the basilica, an aisled building big enough to hold large assemblies. At each end there might be a raised dais [platform] where the city magistrates presided over their courts.[46]

The characteristic stone arches of a Roman aqueduct remain nearly intact after almost two thousand years; (below) equally well preserved are the paving stones in this section of the famous Via Appia.

Other typical public buildings included religious temples, large bathhouses, theaters, and amphitheaters, or arenas for public games. Surrounding these were *domus*, or private houses, and *insulae*, blocks of crowded apartment buildings; and meandering through them all were aqueducts, tall stone structures that carried water from the countryside into town. Connecting a city to neighboring towns were *viae*, paved public roads, such as the renowned Via Appia, or Appian Way, stretching some 366 miles north-south through central and southern Italy. By the fourth century A.D., the Romans had built more than 53,000 miles of such roads. And all of them, as the famous adage reminds us, led back to Rome, the political and economic hub of both the Republic and the Empire.

An Unceasing Flow of People

What had begun a millennium before as an obscure group of crude farmers' shacks had become, by the era of the *Pax Romana*, the capital and greatest tourist attraction of the known world. Certainly, the city built on seven hills—the Aventine, Caelian, Esquiline, Viminal, Quirinal, Palatine, and Capitoline—was a place like no other. Because it was so ancient and had undergone so many cycles of building and rebuilding, and also because it was so large and populous, Rome was far less ordered than smaller Roman cities. Most of its thousands of streets were chaotic, winding, and narrow (usually less than sixteen feet wide); and its buildings, ranging from stately temples and wealthy *domus* to squalid *insulae, tabernae* (small shops), and *thermopolii* (cheap snack bars), were all jumbled together with little or no thought to planning. In his great study of Roman life, historian Jerome Carcopino offered this colorful description of the sights and sounds of a typical daytime street scene:

By day there reigned intense animation, a breathless jostle, an infernal din. The *tabernae* were crowded as soon as they opened and spread their displays into the street. Here barbers shaved their customers . . . hawkers [peddlers] . . . passed along, bartering their packets of sulfur matches for glass trinkets. Elsewhere, the owner of a cook-shop [*thermopolium*], hoarse with calling to deaf ears, displayed his sausages piping hot in their saucepan. Schoolmasters and their pupils shouted themselves hoarse in the open air. On the one hand, a money-changer rang his coins . . . on a dirty table, on another a beater of gold dust pounded with his shining mallet on his well-worn stone. . . . The flow of pedestrians was unceasing . . . [as] in sun or shade a whole world of people came and went, shouted, squeezed, and thrust through narrow lanes.[47]

The first-century A.D. poet Juvenal left a flustered eyewitness account of these street crowds: "We are blocked by a dense mass of people pressing in on us from behind: one man digs an elbow into me, another a hard litter-pole; one bangs a beam, another a

An Ascending Chain of Command

In the huge, crowded, and disorganized city of Rome, large renovation and building projects, as well as everyday administration and maintenance, were herculean tasks. To make the jobs of the builders, aediles, and other workers and public officials easier, in the late first century B.C. Augustus Caesar ordered that Rome be organized into fourteen districts called *regiones*. Each district further broke down into several *vici*, similar to wards or precincts in modern cities. There were more than two hundred *vici* in all, each *vicus* managed by four local administrators known as *magistri*, who were chosen annually by the residents of their respective wards.

This reorganization program was motivated as much by politics as by logistics. The local ward elections were one way that Augustus tried to emphasize the continuity of republican institutions in the autocratic state he was building and to give the people the feeling that they had some say in how they were governed. In reality, the *magistri* of the city wards had little real authority. They largely followed orders and guidelines issued by higher officials, who, through an ascending chain of command, carried out Augustus's policies.

Merchants, shoppers, soldiers, and slaves swarm through one of Rome's narrow streets. The first-century A.D. poet Juvenal left behind detailed descriptions of such city crowds in his Satires.

wine-cask, against my head. My legs are plastered with mud; soon huge feet trample on me from every side, and a soldier plants his nail-studded shoe firmly on my toe."[48]

The incessant street noise barely decreased at night, when hordes of workers drove horse-drawn carts filled with food and merchandise to replenish the shops, inns, taverns, and snack bars.[49] A frustrated Juvenal complained, "How much sleep, I ask you, can one get in lodgings here? . . . The wagons thundering past through those narrow twist-

ing streets, the cries of drivers caught in a traffic-jam . . . would suffice to jolt the doziest . . . Emperor into permanent wakefulness."[50]

Because there were no streetlights, many nighttime avenues and alleyways were also unsafe. *Sicarii*, or murderers, as well as muggers and burglars, roamed at will, and usually only rich people who could afford gangs of bodyguards armed with torches and weapons dared to venture out after dark. When the less well-to-do Juvenal did so alone he was

Symbol of the Roman Spirit

One of the most sacred and important monuments in Rome was the Capitolium, or Temple of Jupiter, located at the summit of the Capitoline hill and dedicated to the Capitoline Triad, which consisted of the deities Jupiter, Juno, and Minerva. The first version of the building was erected in the sixth century B.C. when Rome was still under Etruscan rule. An Etruscan king, perhaps the last, Tarquinius Superbus, supervised a workforce of Roman plebs in the erection of a temple to Jupiter nearly 200 feet long and 170 feet wide. Jupiter was originally an Etruscan god but the Romans had long before adopted him and placed him at the head of their own religious pantheon of deities.

Rebuilt and expanded many times, the final version of the Capitolium, finished in the first century A.D., was composed almost completely of white marble. Inside the cella, or main room, rested a huge gold and ivory statue of Jupiter, while side chambers featured statues of Juno and Minerva. Outside, above the front pediment, or triangular gable, was a large bronze sculpture depicting Jupiter riding in a quadrigarum, a chariot drawn by four horses. About this special building, Italian scholar Leonardo B. Dal Maso writes in his book Rome of the Caesars: "Throughout the ancient era, it remained the most important temple in the city and became the supreme symbol of the Roman spirit, so much so that each Roman municipality in Italy and in the provinces had its own Capitolium."

The magnificent Capitolium, resting on the summit of the sacred Capitoline hill, as it appeared in the early Empire.

mugged and beaten. Augustus instituted a force of three thousand well-armed police, the *cohortes urbanae*, but the few hundred of their number on the night shift were capable of patrolling only small sections of the huge, sprawling city.

The Spectacle of Rome

Part of what so distinguished Rome from other cities were its many public structures, nearly all of them built on a grand scale. Its arenas and racetracks accommodated tens and even hundreds of thousands of spectators. Dozens of temples with majestic, beautifully decorated colonnades and gigantic porches of gleaming marble towered above the fray of the teeming streets. In addition to the original forum, the Forum Romanum, other larger and more elaborate forums sprang up, including those dedicated to Julius Caesar and the emperors Augustus and Vespasian. The most magnificent of all was the Forum of Trajan, built in the second century A.D., which contained a central plaza measuring 300 by 375 feet and a basilica 500 feet long and 100 feet wide. In addition, Rome had many massive *pons*, or bridges, spanning the Tiber. These were so well built that five of them, including the Pons Aelius and Pons Cestius, are still in use and daily bear with ease the weight of thousands of modern automobiles.

To meet the drinking, cooking, washing, and sewage needs of more than a million people, Rome's aqueducts were also numerous and grand. The Aqua Alexandrina, for instance, channeled a huge stream of water day and night from springs fourteen miles distant. Together, Rome's aqueducts delivered at least 200 million gallons of water to the city each day, enough to supply each resident with 200 gallons.[51]

Thus, though crowded, noisy, and sometimes unsafe, Rome was nonetheless an imposing, stately, and wondrous place that often left first-time visitors awestruck. The

It was panoramic views like this one—of huge, stately public buildings in the heart of Rome—that the Greek traveler Strabo called spectacular and unforgettable.

Citizens, slaves, senators, and merchants are depicted in this reconstructed scene from the Forum Romanum in the late first century B.C.

Greek geographer Strabo, who saw the city in the early first century A.D., later wrote:

> If one should go to the Old Forum [Forum Romanum] and see one forum after another ranged beside it, with their basilicas and temples, and then see the Capitol [Capitoline hill, topped with impressive temples] and the great works of art on it and the Palatine [site of the imperial residences] . . . it would be easy to forget the world outside.

The panorama of Rome at its height, Strabo raved, was "a spectacle from which it is hard to tear yourself away."[52]

Lifestyles of the Haves and Have-Nots: Homes and Their Contents

While the forums, basilicas, temples, amphitheaters, and other large gathering places were the focus of Roman public and social life, the home was the private domain of the family. Then as now the size, style, and features of Roman homes varied considerably according to the wealth and social status of the owners or renters. Most farmers, whether independent or tenant, were poor; so they lived in humble dwellings with few comforts. Their poor counterparts in the cities dwelled in crowded rented apartments in the *insulae*, which were also spare of comforts and conveniences. By contrast, the well-to-do resided in both their spacious urban *domus*, which by the last century of the Republic were elaborately furnished and decorated, and the comfortable country villas to which they escaped from time to time. Because of the stark differences between rich and poor homes, their occupants' cooking, eating, and sanitary habits often varied considerably, as well.

Farmhouses Versus Villas

Fed up with living among "the cruel city's many perils," Juvenal advised his readers to "purchase a freehold house in the country. What it will cost you is no more than you pay in annual rent for some shabby and ill-lit garret [slum] here." What *did* the poet pay for his quarters in a crowded city tenement? In the first century B.C. the average annual rent for such lodgings was two thousand sesterces, so by Juvenal's time, over a century later, four thousand to eight thousand sesterces is not unlikely. For that amount, a person could expect to buy nothing better than a poor farmhouse, the typical abode of a large proportion of the population of the ancient Mediterranean world. Such dwellings were usually small one-, two-, or three-room cottages or shacks built of stone, wood, or thatch. Most had dirt floors, few furnishings, and a central hearth for both heating and cooking. Evidently Juvenal advocated trading one poor hovel for another in order to gain peace and quiet and the satisfaction of owning one's own place. "It's quite an achievement," he wrote, "even out in the backwoods, to have made yourself master of—well, say one lizard, even."[53]

What the writer would surely have preferred was a larger, better-built, and more comfortable villa. Inside, writes scholar Susan McKeever, such country manors were beautifully decorated with mosaics [pictures and designs made of colored tiles], fine furniture, and paintings. Outside, there were well-tended gardens, fountains, and statues. Few villas existed without surrounding farms. These huge estates were self-sufficient, with everything from food and wine to bakeries and bathhouses.[54]

Pliny the Younger had a villa about seventeen miles from Rome on the coast near Ostia, a home he described in a letter to a friend as "large enough for my convenience, without being expensive to maintain."[55] This and similar remarks suggest that his was a rather modest villa for a Roman notable. Yet in the same letter he went on to describe his foyer, four dining rooms, two drawing rooms, parlor, library, at least five bedrooms, four bathing rooms, servants' quarters, adjoining cottage with study and bedroom, wide terrace with gardens, and tennis court!

Pliny's was not the only fine residence in what was clearly a fashionable resort area. He mentioned another villa located between his house and the nearest village, a "little place" with "no less than three public baths" and stocking "all common necessaries." His breathtaking view of the shoreline took in other, even larger villas belonging to members of the privileged classes. "The whole coast is beautifully diversified," he added, "by the adjoining or detached villas that are spread upon it, which whether you are traveling along the sea or the shore, have the effect of a series of towns [seen at a distance]."[56]

Like a House of Cards

Pliny's pleasant seaside retreat represented a world of comfort and solitude that Juvenal could only dream about and envy. The poet had to be content with his tiny apartment in the Subura, a huge mass of run-down *insulae* composing Rome's poorest and most densely populated neighborhood. In fact, the vast majority of the city's inhabitants lived in such tenement blocks. A surviving fourth-century A.D. public record lists 46,602 *insulae* in Rome, compared with only 1,797 private *domus*.

The front side of a typical *insula* was perhaps 250 to 350 feet wide. Its ground floor housed rows of small shops, taverns, and snack bars. Each of the upper floors usually had five to ten individual one- or two-room apartments, called *cenaculae*.[57] Most *insulae* were at least three to five stories high; the

Fine, detailed mosaics, like this depiction of a she-ass nursing lion cubs, graced the floors and walls of both the villas and townhouses of the Roman upper classes.

Perhaps the ultimate Roman villa was that built between A.D. 118 and 138 by the emperor Hadrian at Tivoli, then a lovely rural area a few miles southeast of Rome. Plagued by frequent ill health, this capable ruler spent most of his later years at the villa, which was actually a gigantic complex of structures and gardens rather than a single building; nearly a mile long, it was larger than many small Roman towns. In addition to Hadrian's vast suites of living quarters, the Tivoli villa featured a luxurious bathhouse, a gymnasium, a sports stadium, libraries, guest houses, temples, two theaters, many wide sculpted gardens, and an artificial lake surrounded by splendid colonnades and priceless statues. Many sections of the complex were carefully fashioned to represent real Greek locales. This was because Hadrian was an ardent fan of Greek architecture, art, literature, and language, so much so in fact that in his own time he earned the affectionate nickname "the little Greek."

Unfortunately, today all that is left of this magnificent pleasure palace is ruins. "Columns, marbles . . . floors and even the bricks were carried off," writes Leonardo B. Dal Maso in *Rome of the Caesars*. "Its works of art, searched for since the end of the 15th century, have been scattered throughout the museums of Europe."

A noseless bust of the learned emperor Hadrian (A.D. 76–138), who built what was perhaps history's largest and most splendid country villa.

poet Martial lived for a while on the third floor of an *insula* near the Quirinal hill and mentioned neighbors who had to climb far more stairs than he did. Some evidence suggests that tenant blocks rising six and seven stories were not uncommon. And the tallest of all, the famous Insula of Felicula, erected perhaps in the second century A.D., was very likely ten or more stories high, making it the skyscraper of its day.

Not surprisingly, lacking the metal skeletons supporting large modern buildings, the most massive *insulae* could not bear such great loads and often collapsed suddenly, killing and injuring hundreds of residents. "What countryman ever bargained . . . for his house collapsing about his ears?" complained Juvenal. "Here we live in a city shored up, for the most part, with cheap stays and props. . . . Our landlords . . . [reassure] the tenants they can sleep secure, when all the time the building is poised like a house of cards [ready to collapse]." Because the tenants used oil lamps and candles for lighting and wood-burning braziers (metal pots on stands) for heat, fires were a constant and deadly hazard. Juvenal asserted that "fires and midnight panics are not . . . uncommon events. By the time the smoke's got up to your third-floor apartment . . . your downstairs neighbor is roaring for water."[58]

The dangers of fire and collapse were not the only drawbacks of living in *insulae*. They had no running water, so residents had to fetch their water from public fountains and carry it up many flights of stairs. Few rooms had toilets and drainage pipes leading to the public sewers, forcing the majority of people to use the *foricae*, or public latrines, available on the ground floors of most blocks. These facilities, explain scholars Peter James and Nick Thorpe,

Typical apartment blocks of rundown insulae *crowd the foreground of this reconstruction of one of Rome's residential districts.*

were far more public than their modern equivalents, since they weren't divided into cubicles. They were thought of as convenient meeting places, and the Romans felt no embarrassment at chatting to friends there or even swapping dinner invitations. Ten to twenty people could be seated in comfort around three sides of a room. The waste fell into a drain below the seats, to be washed away by running water.[59]

Pistores, *or miller/bakers, grind grain and bake bread in a Roman bakery. Well-preserved remains of such establishments can be seen today in the ruins of Pompeii.*

The Crowded and Dismal Subura

The Subura, where the poet Juvenal lived, was the poorest and most densely populated section of ancient Rome. Located to the east of the Forum Romanum in the low "valley" between the Esquiline and Viminal hills, it was composed almost entirely of cheap, run-down *insulae*, where tens of thousands of people lived in crowded, often unsanitary conditions. Only one landmark, a stone tower called the Turris Mamilia, rose above the dismal monotony of the apartment blocks. Not surprisingly, many of the Subura's inhabitants belonged to groups that found it difficult to rise in Rome's social ranks—foreigners, Jews, poor freedmen and merchants, and actors—who could not afford to live in better sections of the city.

Living in the Subura was often miserable and dangerous. The poorly constructed tenement buildings frequently collapsed or burned down, killing, maiming, or displacing many. There was no running water and the sewage system was apparently inadequate. In his fifth satire, Juvenal describes how fish, having made their way from the Tiber River into the local sewer drains, were "bloated with sewage [and] regular visitors to the cesspools underlying the slums of the Subura." The odors from so much raw sewage, mixed with smoke from oil lamps and hearths and manure dropped everywhere by horses and other animals, must have produced a foul stench, which Juvenal alludes to in his eleventh satire when he dreams of "fleeing the stuffy Subura."

Exchanging dinner invitations in the toilet was so common, in fact, that Martial described the practice in a popular poem:

> For hours, for a whole day, he'll sit
> On every public lavatory seat.
> It's not because he needs a shit:
> He wants to be asked out to eat.[60]

Those who preferred the privacy of home eliminated their wastes into *lasani*, or chamber pots. They then emptied these into vats under stairwells, or, if the neighbors objected to this practice, dumped them into the streets. Juvenal told of the dangers of these foul missiles and other objects falling on passersby, joking, "You may well be deemed a fool . . . if you go out to dinner without having made your will."[61] Some victims sued after receiving such unwelcome dousings. The second-century A.D. jurist Ulpian recorded a legal rule stating that when someone was injured by an object falling out of a house, "the judge shall award to the victim in addition to medical fees . . . necessary to his recovery, the total of the wages of which he has been . . . deprived by the inability to work."[62]

Another drawback of *insulae* was that most of the *cenaculae* within them lacked the luxury of kitchens. Having no way to cook their food, a majority of the urban poor either took it to a local *pistor*, who for a fee tossed it into his oven, or ate out at the *thermopolii* found on every block. Typical fare included hot sausages and other meats, bread, cheese, figs, dates, nuts, cakes, and wine. The huge demand for these cookshops and snack bars is evidenced by their great numbers; considering that, counting those in pubs and taverns, more than two hundred have been excavated in the small city of Pompeii, there must have been close to ten thousand in Rome.

The Realm Within the *Domus*

Because so few of the poorly built *insulae* have survived intact, little is known about how their apartments were subdivided and their rooms laid out. By contrast, many well-preserved *domus* have been excavated, revealing much about how more affluent urban Romans lived. Although these comfortable townhouses varied in size and exact layout, most had the same basic features, including a herm guarding the front doorway. An idea borrowed from the Greeks, this was a pedestal supporting a bust of the Greek god Hermes (whom the Romans called Mercury), protector of travelers, who supposedly dis-couraged evil from entering the house. Many Roman versions featured prominent and realistic representations of the god's genitals, most of which were defaced in the late Empire by zealous Christians who thought them obscene.

A tour of a *domus*'s interior began with a front room, or large foyer, called the atrium, where the paterfamilias visited with his clients in the morning and received his dinner guests at night.[63] Typically, the atrium was decorated elegantly with ornamented columns, expensive statues, tiled mosaics, and wall paintings. According to Johnston, the room "received its light from a central opening in the roof, the *compluvium*, which

This reconstruction of the atrium of a wealthy Roman townhouse shows the open compluvium *above and the* impluvium *catch-basin below it.*

A well-manicured and luxurious Roman garden. For many city dwellers, the garden represented a soothing and essential link with the countryside, the traditional setting of Rome's early tribal society.

derived its name from the fact that rain [*pluvia*], as well as air and light, could enter here. Just beneath this a basin, the *impluvium*, was hollowed out in the floor to catch the water for domestic purposes."[64]

Roman atriums also frequently featured an alcove that held the *lararium*, a small shrine to the family gods and spirits, where members of the household regularly prayed. Near this altar was a cupboard in which the family kept its *imago*, a very lifelike mask, complete with wax skin and a wig, of its most illustrious ancestor. Families with many prominent forebears had several such cupboards. "When a man of the family died," writes scholar Colleen McCullough, "an actor was employed to don the *imago* and impersonate the ancestor. If a man became consul [or distinguished himself in some other way], his mask was made and added to the family collection."[65]

Corridors led away from the atrium to various other rooms. Among these were usually several bedrooms, including one or two used for servants' quarters; the *tablinum*, a study used by the paterfamilias; the kitchen;

the dining room, or *triclinium*; a small bathroom equipped with a toilet that piped wastes into the city sewers (but usually without a tub, as most Romans visited the public baths daily); and a walled garden called the *peristylum*, from which the modern word peristyle is derived.

The pleasant peristyle was perhaps the most popular part of a Roman home; some families set up their altars and *imago* cupboards there rather than in the atrium. Another idea adopted from the Greeks, whose houses were built around central courtyards open to the elements, peristyles were favorite spots in which to relax and enjoy a small slice of nature, in the form of the family gardens. The degree to which Romans loved their manicured and often elaborate gardens is evident in Martial's boast about those at his home in Spain, to which he returned after living for thirty-five years in Rome:

This latticed shade of vine, my conduits [water pipes] and cascade [artificial waterfall], my roses . . . my vegetables . . .

my private tank where tame eels swim, my dove-cote [pigeon house] just as white and trim as its own inmates— everything in the small realm in which I'm king was given me by my patroness and friend, Marcella (whom heaven bless).[66]

Lighting, Heating, and Cooking

While the atrium and gardens of a *domus* served mainly ceremonial and recreational functions, the bedrooms, kitchen, and dining room catered to more practical needs. Most bedrooms and sitting rooms had very little furniture by modern standards, emphasizing instead fine statues, paintings, and mosaics, which gave these chambers an open, airy, and elegant look. The most versatile piece of furniture was the *lectus*, a couch with a padded seat, arm, or head rests, and often pillows and a wooden back, used for sitting, for reclining to eat, and also for sleeping. Various tables, chairs, stools, and storage chests were employed as need and want dictated.

Some furniture items provided light and heat. Oil lamps, called *lucernae*, came in many forms, some resting on tables, others hanging from the ceiling or sitting atop tall bronze stands called *candelabrae*. All of these lamps were, as works of art, says Johnston, "exceedingly beautiful. Even those of the cheapest material were frequently of graceful form and proportions, while to those of costly material the skill of the artist in many cases must have given a value far above that of the rare stones or precious metals of which they were made."[67]

Like *insulae*, *domus* utilized portable charcoal-burning braziers for heat. A few homes, most notably wealthy *domus* and vil-

las in regions that grew cold in the winter, had a more complex heating system known as a hypocaust, invented by businessman Gaius Sergius Orata about 100 B.C. In the most common version of the system, the house was built over a shallow cellar and supported by brick or concrete pillars two to three feet high. Brick channels connected the cellar to a furnace located away from the house. Warm air circulated from the furnace through the channels and gently heated the

Glass for Windows

Over the course of many centuries, the technique of glassmaking slowly spread from ancient Egypt, through Phoenicia (along the coast of Palestine), to other parts of the Mediterranean, including Italy. One result was that in many of the wealthier Roman homes glass began to replace oilcloth, sheepskin, mica, and thinly sliced gypsum as a window covering. According to L. Sprague de Camp in The Ancient Engineers:

"The first panes [introduced during the late Republic] were little round skylights, the glass of which was too irregular and impure for true transparency. But during the first century A.D., glass window-panes of the modern type appeared. By the end of the century, glass factories had become common in Italy and were spreading into Gaul. Even greenhouses were known. The [first-century A.D.] agricultural writer Columella advised raising cucumbers in . . . boxes covered by *speculares* [transparent glass panes]."

A Roman lounges on a lectus, *a multipurpose couch. One of its most common functions was as a recliner on which to rest while consuming the* cena, *the main meal of the day.*

ground floor, and, in the most elaborate versions, also circulated into hollow spaces in some of the walls.

Some additional heat radiated from the kitchen, which usually had both a wide hearth for cooking and a brick-lined oven for baking. Liversidge describes those in one excavated *domus* in the small city of Augst, near what is now Basel, Switzerland (originally in the province of Lower Germany):

> On [the hearth] the cook would place small iron grids and tripods supporting pots and metal vessels over heaps of glowing charcoal. Across the room is a round oven with [a] domed top. This would be heated and then the ashes raked out and the bread or cakes put in.[68]

A typical kitchen also was equipped with large tables for food preparation, as well as shelves and storage bins on which amphorae containing wine and olive oil were stacked. Olive oil amphorae were as common as milk and fruit juice containers are today, graphic proof of which is the discovery in modern

Most Roman oil lamps, like this one, were both useful and decorative. A wick protruded from the front hole.

The Romans kept many kinds of pets in their homes, including dogs, cats, birds, and others common in modern Western societies. However, some of the pets that regularly had the range of Roman houses are found today mainly in the wild or in zoos. These included snakes, valued not only for their rodent-killing prowess but also as a fertility symbol. A household snake was thought to represent the spirit of the paterfamilias (or the materfamilias if a female snake); therefore killing a pet snake was considered unlucky, for it might lead to the father's or mother's injury or death.

Monkeys were another common pet. A popular type was the guenon, a common variety in northern Africa, where the Romans had several provinces by the first century A.D. Hunters captured these animals by the hundreds each year and shipped them, for considerable profits, to Rome and many other cities across the empire. Most monkey owners probably kept their pets on leashes or tethers. Otherwise, the agile, swift creatures easily got away and were difficult to catch. Escapees were often seen climbing up and across household colonnades or cavorting about the city rooftops.

Rome of an ancient rubbish heap composed solely of discarded oil amphorae. Archaeologists estimate that the mound is 3,000 feet around and 140 feet high, and contains the remains of over 40 million jugs!

He Rarely Ate So Well

Food prepared in the kitchen was served in the *triclinium*, where the whole family ate together (except during special banquets and parties, which were usually restricted to adults). In a practice that would seem strange and awkward today, the Romans reclined while eating. Carcopino comments:

Nothing would have induced the Romans of the Empire to eat otherwise. They considered the reclining position indispensable to their physical comfort, but always a mark of elegance and of social distinction. In the old days it was good enough for a woman to eat, seated at her husband's feet. But now that the [more liberated] Roman matron took her place beside the men . . . to eat sitting was suitable only for children, who sat on stools . . . or for slaves, who received permission to recline like their masters only on holidays.[69]

As for the meals themselves, breakfast normally consisted of bread or wheat biscuits, either dipped in wine or covered with honey, along with some cheese, olives, and/or raisins. Lunch, called *prandium* (which many people skipped in favor of a larger dinner), also usually consisted of cold food, including bread, salads, fruits, and leftovers from yesterday's main meal. That meal, the *cena*, most commonly came in the late afternoon. It was served in three courses: the first consisting of appetizers such as salads, oysters, mushrooms, eggs, and sardines; the second comprised of fish, poultry, or pork, the Romans' favorite meat, accompanied by vegetables; and the third, dessert, typically consisting of

At sumptuous banquets like this one, wealthy patricians and equestrians entertained friends and clients. As the popular humorists Juvenal and Martial noted, it was common practice for the hosts to set aside the most expensive and exotic dishes for themselves and to serve cheaper foods to the lower-class clients.

fruit, nuts, and honey cakes. The main drink was wine, which in wealthy homes was chilled with ice. Donkey trains hauled in ice from the nearest mountains to be stored in underground pits until people were ready to use it.

Needless to say, poorer Romans like Juvenal rarely ate so well. Even when invited to dinner at a rich man's house, he received cheap fare while his host kept the best foods for himself. "See now that huge lobster being served to my lord, all garnished with asparagus," he recalled, while he himself got a single shrimp "hemmed in by half an egg—a fit banquet for the dead."[70] In such ways was emphasized the vast gulf that separated the lifestyles of patron and client, *domus* and *insula*, and the Roman haves and have-nots.

"A Bald Head with Dressed Hair": Social Customs and Institutions

I f a modern person could somehow be transported back through time to ancient Rome, he or she would undoubtedly find certain native social customs and habits familiar. After all, many of the social ideas prevalent in modern Western society developed from Roman originals or from Roman versions of Greek originals. For instance, some styles of clothing, hair, and jewelry, as well as many general grooming habits, have changed little over the centuries. Then as now people went to the barber, to the doctor, and to school, and many of the Romans' marriage, child-rearing, and divorce practices were similar to those of the present days.

On the other hand, a modern time traveler in ancient Rome would soon discover many of these similarities to be superficial. It would not take long to see that what *did* change a great deal over the centuries were social attitudes, both personal and public, for the Romans often accepted and took for granted ideas that would surprise, shock, or offend people today. The unashamed and relaxed manner in which they sat together and socialized in public toilets is a perfect example. Also very different were their attitudes toward sexual relationships; ideas about who should be educated and what was most important to learn; and overall sense of humor, which most people today, no doubt, would find unfunny or in poor taste.

A Pain in the *Podex*?

In fact, to modern ears much of everyday Roman humor would seem crude and cruel. Typically, Romans joked in a very blunt, graphic, and often personal manner, thinking nothing of poking fun at the physical shortcomings or misfortunes of others. Not even the supremely educated and humane Cicero was above such ridicule. When his son-in-law Dolabella, an unusually short man, entered a crowded room carrying a large sword, Cicero demanded in a loud voice, "Who has fastened my son-in-law to that sword?"[71] As expected, the onlookers burst into laughter.

Meaner yet were professional humorists such as the widely popular Martial, who regularly kept the Roman masses snickering and chuckling with cruel jests like this one: "The sort of girl I hate is the scrawny one, with arms so thin my rings would fit them. . . . But all the same I don't go in for sheer bulk. I appreciate good meat, not blubber on my plate."[72] Roman parents often thought it funny to name their children using the Latin words for lame, flatfeet, stammerer, fat, boar, ass, pig, onion, chickpea, and so forth, a habit that today would be considered cruel. And at public gatherings, such as banquets, weddings, and parades, it was common practice to hurl back and forth snide and lewd remarks and jokes. Men and women, young and old alike, regularly used the word *podex*, a mild obscenity for the rear end, along with many much more vulgar terms for various private body parts.

Dressing Above One's Means

The use of cruel or sexually explicit humor was only one of many Roman social trends. City dwellers in particular, ever conscious of their social status, were concerned about how they appeared in public. Proper and becoming clothes, hairstyles, makeup, and jewelry were a must for members of the upper classes, as well as for those of lesser means trying to get ahead or make a favorable impression. For example, clients, no matter how poor, always made sure to be well dressed and neatly groomed when visiting their patrons, even if doing so meant going into debt. "In Rome, everyone dresses smartly, above his means," remarked Juvenal. "This failing is universal here: we all live in a state of pretentious [showy] poverty."[73] Martial described a wealthy dinner host who was so clothes conscious that he changed his outfit eleven times during a single banquet.

The most fashionable article of clothing was the toga, which consisted of a large oblong piece of cloth wrapped around the body in complicated folds and drapes. For many centuries only citizens enjoyed the privilege of wearing the toga, but that restriction relaxed a bit during the Empire. Even then, different kinds of togas denoted different social or political ranks. An average citizen wore the plain white *toga alba*; senators and other high officials the *toga praetexta*, which featured a purple border; a triumphant general the all-purple, gold-trimmed *toga picta*; and mourners attending a funeral the black *toga pulla*. In the early Republic, women also wore the toga for formal wear

This statue of Sabina, wife of the emperor Hadrian, depicts her wearing a draped palla, *or cloak.*

but over time they adopted instead a draped outer cloak called the *palla*.

The most common casual garment was the simple tunic, made from two rectangular pieces of cloth stitched up the sides. Men and women alike wore it knee length, and many women wore an ankle-length dress, the *stola*, over their tunic. People of both genders and all ages also wore cloaks, scarves, and hats when fashion or the weather dictated. Decorative fastening pins called fibulae held cloaks, scarves, togas, and other garments in place at the shoulder. In extremely casual surroundings, such as at the public baths or the beach, men often wore a simple wool or linen loincloth and some women wore bikinis almost exactly like those worn today. The *crepida*, or sandal, which came in a wide variety of shapes and styles, was a popular footwear in the warm Mediterranean climate; however, canvas and leather shoes and boots were quite common, as well.

The "Poufed" Look

The Romans considered grooming, especially hairstyles and makeup, to be just as important to overall appearance as proper clothes. Influenced by the fashion in the Greek kingdoms, men wore beards and long hair in the early Republic. However, in the late Republic and early Empire they maintained short hair and the clean-shaven look. The *tonsor*, or barber, became so important to men that many wealthy households kept one or more *tonsores* in their permanent employ. The majority who could not afford this luxury went to their local barbershop, or *tonstrina*, which served both grooming and social functions. Carcopino comments:

> The *tonstrina* became a rendezvous, a club, a gossip shop, an inexhaustible dispensary of information, a place for arranging interviews and the like. . . . The hairdresser's shop was surrounded with benches on which the waiting clients sat.

Mirrors hung on the walls so that customers might give themselves a critical glance on leaving the chair.[74]

Some barbers came to specialize in the use of curling irons that gave men sculptured, "poufed" hairdos that Martial saw as overdone in young men and downright ridiculous in older men trying to look young. "Will you please," he begged of one of the latter, "confess yourself old, so as after all to appear so? Nothing is more unsightly than a bald head with dressed hair."[75]

Women were even more obsessed than men with grooming. In the early Republic women usually arranged their long hair in buns; but later, as they became more socially liberated, they adopted a wide range of styles, including the curled and poufed hairdos popular with some men, and also wore wigs made of slaves' hair. Jewelry—typically gold chains, bracelets, and anklets; rings with

This wild, poufed hairstyle was popular with many Roman women during the early Empire.

His Outlandish Behavior

Although wearing plenty of makeup was customary for Roman women in the Empire, perhaps the most famous user of elaborate makeup was a man—Elagabalus. Hailing from Syria, where he served as priest of an eastern sun god, he became emperor in A.D. 218 at the age of fifteen and immediately shocked conservative Romans with his outlandish behavior. According to an account attributed to an ancient biographer named Aelius Lampridius (quoted in *Lives of the Later Caesars*), "He sold both honors and ranks and pow-

ers, both in person and through his slaves and agents of his lusts. . . . Many [both male and female] whose bodies had pleased him he took from the stage, circus, and amphitheater to the court." In addition to engaging in various overt sexual acts with these people as part of his religious ceremonies, Elagabalus often dressed as a woman, wore huge earrings and strings of pearls, and painted his eyes with gold makeup, his lips with blue, and his cheeks and feet with red. "He used to make his face to look like a painting of Venus," wrote Lampridius, "and was depilated [had the hair removed] all over his body—thinking that it was the principal enjoyment of life to appear worthy and suited for the lusts of the greatest number." Because of these and numerous other outrageous excesses, after only four years in power the colorful but unpopular young ruler was murdered by his own guards, who dragged his body through the city streets and then dumped it into the Tiber.

A statue of the controversial young emperor Elagabalus, whose outrageous grooming habits and sexual excesses shocked many Romans.

precious gems set in gold or silver; and earrings of gold, silver, bronze, pearl, and emerald—was a must for well-to-do women. Poorer women had to content themselves with fake gems fashioned of colored glass.

Roman women also wore what most people today would consider a great deal of makeup. They used a chalklike powder to make their complexions stylishly pale, painted their lips and cheeks red, and lined their eyes and eyebrows with black *stibium*, pow-

dered antimony mixed with water. Martial poked fun at one woman's painted, artificial look, saying that "your hair [a wig] is at the hairdresser's; you . . . sleep tucked away in a hundred cosmetics boxes . . . [and] wink at men under an eyebrow which you took out of a drawer."[76] Indeed, the makeup table of a typical middle-class or wealthy woman was crammed with razors, brushes, hair nets, wigs, and jars of creams, pastes, oils, colored dyes, and perfumes.[77]

Love, Marriage, and Divorce

One of the main objects of having nice clothes and a well-groomed appearance, particularly for younger people, was to look attractive to the opposite sex. However, the majority of marriages, or *matrimonii* (singular, *matrimonium*), were not the result of falling in love, but rather were arranged by parents for political, social, and business reasons. As Paul Veyne puts it, in Rome

> the household [was] the household, and husband and wife each [had] their respective duties to perform. If they [happened] to get on well together, so much the better; but mutual understanding [was] not essential. . . . Marriage was one thing, happy couples were another.

Love in marriage was a stroke of good fortune; it was not the basis of the institution.[78]

Of course, when love *was* the foundation of a relationship, the feelings of mutual attraction, desire, respect, and tenderness were no less profound than those experienced by modern lovers. "Love, let us live as we lived," wrote the fourth-century A.D. poet Ausonius to his beloved wife, "nor lose the little names that were the first night's grace. And never come the day that sees us old, I still your lad, and you my little lass."[79]

Whether graced by true love or not, Roman weddings were important and festive occasions. Typically, a couple first became betrothed, or engaged, at a meeting in which the parents discussed the bride's dowry, the

The strong, loving bond some Roman couples enjoyed is captured in this charming roundel, bearing busts of a husband and wife surrounded by the inscription: "May you grow old together."

A sheep is prepared for sacrifice during a Roman wedding ceremony. Guided by the maid of honor, the bride and groom join hands (at right), symbolizing their new union.

money or property she would bring into the marriage that would benefit her husband. An exchange of gifts and rings and the signing of a contract took place at this time.

On the wedding day itself, the groom, his relatives, and the other guests marched in procession to the bride's home, where she waited dressed in a white tunic and orange-red veil, with flowers in her hair. A bridesmaid stepped forward and joined the couple's hands, after which everyone said a prayer to the gods and a second contract was signed. Then there was a feast that went on well into the evening, when finally everyone led the bride, now a *marita*, or wife, and the groom, now a *maritus*, or husband, to his house, where he carried her over the threshold.

Many Roman marriages, begun with such gaiety and optimism, ultimately ended in divorce. In the first few centuries of the Republic divorce was very rare; but by the early Empire more liberal social attitudes and the enhanced status and rights of women had made divorce quite common. In an era in which it was not unusual for a woman, partic-

ularly an upper-class one, to marry three or more times, the witty Seneca quipped, "No woman need blush to break off her marriage since the most illustrious ladies have adopted the practice of reckoning the year . . . by [the names of] their husbands. They divorce in order to re-marry. They marry in order to divorce."[80]

Schools and the Proper Orator

Another social institution that began with men and women interacting and eventually led to their parting company was school. Young boys and girls from families who could afford it went to a *ludus*, or private elementary school, which was supported by their parents rather than the state. Children from most poor families were not able to attend school and usually remained illiterate. At a typical school, which consisted of a single rented room, often in the rear of a shop, the teacher, known as a *magister*, taught basic reading and writing skills to about twelve

Cicero, the Master of Rhetoric

In his famous study of Roman culture, Caesar and Christ, *the great historian Will Durant gave the following description of Cicero's legendary mastery of rhetoric and oratory.*

"The fifty-seven orations that have come down to us from Cicero illustrate all the tricks of successful eloquence. They excel in the passionate presentation of one side of a question or a character . . . the appeal to vanity, prejudice, sentiment, patriotism, and piety, the ruthless exposure of the real or reported, public or private, faults of the opponent or his client, the skillful turning of attention from unfavorable points, the barrage of rhetorical questions framed to make answer difficult or damaging. . . . These speeches do not pretend to be fair; they are defamations rather than declamations, briefs that take every advantage of that freedom of abuse which, though forbidden to the stage, was allowed in the Forum and the courts. Cicero does not hesitate to apply to his victims terms like 'swine,' 'pest,' 'butcher,' 'filth' . . . [and his] orations abound rather with egotism and rhetoric than in moral sincerity [or] philosophical wisdom. . . . But what eloquence! . . . Certainly no man before or after Cicero spoke Latin so seductively charming and fluent, so elegantly passionate; this was the zenith of Latin prose."

Marcus Tullius Cicero delivers a speech. He opposed the policies of the dictator Julius Caesar, whose younger cohort, Mark Antony, eventually had the great orator murdered.

students at a time. Some of these pupils were accompanied by a *paedagogus*, a family slave or freedman who walked them to class and supervised their behavior.

About the age of eleven, girls generally left school. Some continued their education at home using private tutors, but most began preparing for marriage, which most often occurred when they were about fourteen or fifteen. Boys, on the other hand, went on to secondary school, called *schola* (or *grammaticus*). There, they studied geometry, geography, history, and music, and also learned to read and write Greek, since Greek civilization had such a profound influence on all aspects of Roman life.

The primary function of secondary school, however, was to prepare young men for the study of rhetoric, the art of persuasive speech and public oratory. This skill was considered absolutely essential for the educated man, especially if he expected to go into law or politics, the two most prestigious professions. Colleen McCullough comments:

> A proper orator spoke according to carefully laid-out rules and conventions which extended far beyond mere words; body movements and gestures were an intrinsic [essential] part of it. . . . It must be remembered that the audience which gathered to listen to public oration, be it concerned with politics or the law courts . . . watched and listened in a spirit of marked criticism, for they knew all the rules and the techniques . . . and were not easy to please.[81]

Rhetoric and its rigid disciplines, which taught a person to argue a position exhaustively whether it was right or wrong or true or false, remained the ideal goal of Roman edu-

Bored by Science

That the Romans, unlike the Greeks, lacked interest in and largely ignored and neglected scientific research had a profound effect on world history. In the last few centuries B.C., Greek scientists had originated much scientific theory, including the realization that the earth is a sphere, and had conducted many experiments, among them measuring the circumference of that sphere with fair accuracy. Observing the shadows cast by sticks standing vertically in two different latitudes, the third-century B.C. Greek astronomer Eratosthenes, who lived and worked in Alexandria, Egypt, used geometry and shrewd deduction to work out the earth's circumference. His estimate was within 1 percent of the true value. Another Alexandrian Greek, a first-century A.D. engineer named Hero, described what was apparently a crude precursor of the steam engine, consisting of a hollow ball that rotated on a column of hot air generated by a pot of boiling water. Hero also described a small windmill that ran a pipe organ and other ingenious devices.

Had the practical and determined Romans seized upon the Greek initiative, devoted the proper time and resources, and elaborated on existing mechanical devices, there is little doubt that they could have created an industrial revolution nearly two thousand years ahead of its time. In a way, then, James Watt, modern inventor of the steam engine, achieved success and changed the world in wondrous ways because the Romans were bored by science.

cation right up to the end of the Empire. The unfortunate result was that higher education focused narrowly on literary topics and almost entirely ignored many important realms of knowledge. "In general," writes Michael Grant, "the ready-made sets of arguments . . . employed in rhetorical courses excluded observation and experience, destroyed curiosity, and blunted distinctions between true and false. Particularly disastrous was the exclusion of science from the curriculum."[82]

Doctors and Medicine

Indeed, Roman civilization produced few original scientific thinkers. Seneca did turn out the *Quaestiones Naturales*, a volume in which he offered natural explanations for phenomena such as rain, wind, comets, and earthquakes. And he correctly maintained that later generations would open up vast new realms of discovery: "How many things our sons will learn that we cannot now suspect! . . . Our descendants will marvel at our ignorance."[83] Yet for the most part Seneca borrowed his ideas from Greek scientists long dead and his book was riddled with references to omens as well as speeches on morality.

Pliny the Elder made a more serious and systematic attempt to list and explain the wonders of nature in his *Natural History*, stating in the preface, "My purpose is to give a general description of everything that is known to exist throughout the earth."[84] To his credit, he nearly succeeded. His massive one-man encyclopedia dealt with some 20,000 separate topics and cited as references more than 2,000 volumes by 473 authors (most of whom were Greeks whose works are now lost). But like Seneca, Pliny did not offer

much in the way of original or illuminating scientific ideas. Pliny also gathered and passed on numerous superstitions, apparently believing, for instance, that a menstruating woman's touch caused seeds to turn sterile.

The only scientific discipline into which the Romans delved was medicine, the practice of which became an important social institution that touched everyone's life at one time or another. The better Roman doctors, who inherited much of their knowledge from the Greeks, attempted to treat a wide variety of ailments. Using specialized surgical instruments (more than two hundred different varieties were discovered at Pompeii), they removed tonsils; repaired hernias and fractured bones; performed abortions, simple dentistry, and eye operations; and even did rudimentary plastic surgery. A Roman army surgeon's tomb excavated in Germany yielded a brain surgery kit that contained, among other useful instruments, a bronze drill for opening the skull. Roman physicians were especially skilled at making false limbs. James and Thorpe report:

> A skeleton with a remarkably well modeled artificial leg was discovered in a tomb of ca. 300 B.C. at Capua in central Italy. The leg was made of wood sheathed in two thin bronze sheets, which were attached to the wooden core by an iron pin. It was concave at the top to hold the surviving stump of the thigh, and would have reached from the knee to the ankle. A separate wooden foot was probably attached at the base, but this has not survived.[85]

It must be noted that only some doctors were highly skilled and that those who were not caused the death of many patients. Also, many quack doctors continued to advocate traditional remedies, such as reciting weird incantations and mystical numbers, or consuming magic well water, gladiator's blood, human fat, or other ineffective substances.

Nevertheless, an impressive and reasonably effective medical establishment made up of skilled, caring, and dedicated physicians developed during the Empire, thanks in large degree to state-sponsored medical schools started by the emperor Vespasian in the late first century A.D. Also, the ever-dependable shelter of Roman law helped to raise standards and weed out quacks. For instance, the *lex Aquilia* held doctors responsible for negligence and the *lex Cornelia* severely punished them if their carelessness caused a patient to die. Such laws, along with those relating to marriage, divorce, and other social institutions, foreshadowed similar versions in later cultures, including our own.

CHAPTER 6

Bread and Circuses: Leisure Pursuits and Entertainments

Many modern novels and movies have portrayed the majority of Romans as drunken revelers cavorting at sumptuous banquets or as mindless masses screaming and laughing in frenzied bloodlust at chariot races and gladiator fights. Such depictions, suggesting that Romans spent much of their time engaged in excess and frivolity, are exaggerated and misleading. First, lavish feasts and parties were largely given and attended by members of the upper classes. The majority of Romans were poor and either could not afford to stage or were not invited to such festivities.

Second, while Rome's theaters and stadiums were almost always full, their seating capacities were tiny compared with the city's population. For example, the largest theater in the city, the Theater of Marcellus, seated only 14,000 people. The famous Colosseum arena held some 50,000 spectators, yet that accounted for less than one-twentieth of the city's inhabitants. And although the largest stadium of all, the Circus Maximus, accommodated about 250,000 people, perhaps a quarter of Rome's population, it presented chariot races only about seventeen days a year in the early Empire. The average citizen could expect to find a seat in the "Great Circus" on only a few of those days. Even assuming that person managed to find seats in various other theaters and arenas from time to time, he or she probably enjoyed such large-scale entertainments on only a small number of Rome's many public holidays. As Balsdon writes:

> We ourselves see nothing wrong with the idea of a man who, with two nonworking days a week, gives himself the enjoyment on one of those days of watching racing [or] football. . . . We should be wise to observe the same sense of proportion before we pass . . . judgment on the Roman who, at the start of the Empire, can only have spent a few more days than seventeen a year in such indulgence.[86]

This does not mean that the average Roman did not enjoy leisure time. In addition to the big public shows, there were numerous religious festivals, clan get-togethers, weddings, and dinner parties one could attend. When they could afford to, some individuals left the city to go hunting or fishing. And just as people do today, everyday Romans often organized their own street games, including ball games similar to tennis, board games akin to chess and checkers, and also various kinds of gambling, including *talis*, or tossing dice, and *micatio*. In the latter (played as *morra* in modern Italy), two players repeatedly raised random numbers of fingers and simultaneously guessed the totals until one guessed right and won whatever had been bet.

The Roman Baths

Perhaps the most common leisure pastime of all, one enjoyed by Romans of nearly all walks of life, was a visit to the *thermarum* (plural, *thermae*), or public bath. The first bathhouses, at the time privately run, appeared in Rome in the second century B.C. By Augustus's reign the city boasted more than 170 private *thermae*, and in the first century A.D. various emperors began building large public versions. The baths became so important an institution that most people attended one daily or at least a few times a week instead of bathing at home. Even the poor could afford to go often, since the entrance fee was minimal—a *quadrans*, perhaps equivalent to about a penny or less today. Children were admitted free. Most bathhouses either offered separate facilities for women or staggered their hours so that men and women attended at different times.

The larger *thermae* were huge, beautifully decorated buildings with complex and ingenious hot and cold water systems. Johnston writes that they provided

A reconstruction of a section of the magnificent baths erected by the emperor Caracalla in the third century A.D.

a room for undressing and dressing (*apodyterium*) . . . furnished with benches and often with compartments for the clothes; the warm anteroom (*tepidarium*), in which the bather waited long enough for the perspiration to start; . . . the hot room (*caldarium*), for the hot bath; the cold room (*frigidarium*) for the cold bath; the room for rubbing . . . with oil that finished the bath (*unctorium*), from which the bather returned into the *apodyterium* for his clothes.[87]

Many bathhouses also had a swimming pool and a *laconicum*, or sauna. The sauna, warm pools, floors, and sometimes even the walls were heated by large hypocaust systems driven by oversized furnaces attended by slaves.

But the *thermae* were much more than places where Romans perspired, washed, and swam. They were, according to Susan McKeever, "busy social centers, where people could exercise, chat, play games, do business, or even have their legs waxed [a practice in which even some men indulged]."[88] Indeed, in addition to its extensive bathing facilities, a large public bath featured massage parlors and hair salons; indoor and outdoor exercise rooms and gyms, called *palaestrae*, where people played handball and *harpastum*, a rough-and-tumble ball game similar to rugby, lifted weights, and wrestled (women wrestlers were not uncommon); snack bars and gift shops; gardens for strolling and leisure conversation; and even libraries and reading rooms. Combining many features of modern malls and social clubs, the *thermae* were places where people could enjoy themselves for a pleasant hour or an entire day.

Appealing, Bizarre, and Disgusting?

Many Romans liked attending the baths in the late afternoon so that after exerting themselves they could immediately enjoy the welcome reward of a good supper. For people of lesser means this meant a quick visit to a cookshop, followed by the walk home, an hour or two conversing with family or friends, and then bed. By contrast, for the well-to-do and any of their clients fortunate enough to be invited, there were splendid dinner parties lasting well into the evenings nearly every day of the week. Often, these luxurious gatherings featured dozens of rich foods, slaves to wait on the guests hand and foot, and live entertainment, including singers, dancers, acrobats, and poets reciting their works.

Naturally, people were eager to land invitations to such parties. Martial described one particularly desperate fellow: "When Selius spreads his nets for an invitation to dinner, if you're due to plead a case in court . . . take him along. He'll furnish your applause: 'Well said!' 'Bravo!' [and so on], till you say 'Shut up now, you've earned your food.'"[89] Martial himself was upset whenever a patron or moneyed acquaintance failed to extend him an invitation. "Because you're always giving splendid dinners and never ask me," he chided, "I've planned my revenge. I'm so offended by now that if you beg me, 'please come to my house' on bended knees, I'll . . . what will I do to you? Arrive."[90]

From a modern perspective, the feasts that Martial and the others were so eager to attend would seem at once appealing, bizarre, and probably disgusting. On the positive side, the food was beautifully prepared and no doubt delicious, the entertainment

Many Roman banquets featured live entertainment, including musicians, dancers, poets reciting their works, wrestlers, and occasionally, as depicted here, fighting warriors.

Trimalchio's Feast

The extreme luxury and exotic foods featured at dinner parties in some of the wealthier Roman homes were captured for posterity by the first-century A.D. writer Petronius in "Trimalchio's Feast," from his *Satyricon* (quoted in *The Portable Roman Reader*), in which the host, Trimalchio, offers up a particularly lavish dish.

A course was served whose peculiarity attracted everyone's attention; for a double tray in which it was set had the twelve signs of the Zodiac arranged in a circle and over each sign [was] some kind of food that was appropriate to it—over the Ram, some chick-peas with tendrils that curled like ram's horns; over the Bull, a bit of beef . . . over the Lion, an African fig. . . . An Egyptian slave passed us some bread in a silver bread-plate, while Trimalchio croaked out a popular song from the musical farce called *The Garlic Eater*.

Juvenal also described some of the richer foods enjoyed by Roman notables. In his eleventh satire, he mentioned that a "splendid banquet" might include such items as "sow's paunch, pheasant, boar, antelope, hare, gazelle, not to mention the tall flamingo."

In this detail from a wall painting found in Pompeii, a servant carries an elegantly prepared food tray during a banquet.

This carved relief of a reveler clutching a wine cup captures the casual, jovial air of Roman banquets.

ment of the feast, some diners induced vomiting: Juvenal told of one especially repulsive woman who "souses the floor with the washings of her insides. . . . She drinks and vomits like a big snake that has tumbled into a vat."[92]

The Play Was Not the Thing

Another leisure pursuit, the theater, like so many other cultural aspects of Roman life, was inspired almost entirely by the Greeks, who originated the art form in the sixth and fifth centuries B.C. The Romans were slow to catch on, and formal plays were not presented in Rome until the third century B.C. Then, and with few exceptions for centuries to come, Roman playwrights turned out copies of Greek originals, imitating their themes, plots, and stock characters, and even giving most of these characters Greek names.

Nevertheless, some Roman playwrights, particularly Plautus and Terence, who wrote in the second century B.C., were very talented and their works became widely popular. Plautus usually kept his audiences rolling in the aisles with slapstick comedies such as *The Pot of Gold*, *The Braggart Warrior*, and *The Comedy of Asses*. Writes historian Lionel Casson:

> To Plautus, the play was not the thing; the audience was. The customers were rude Romans who had come to laugh from the belly, and he did his level best to accommodate them. . . . At all costs he kept the pot of the action boiling, the stream of gags and puns . . . flowing swiftly and steadily.[93]

Plautus and his contemporaries had to be content with producing their works in makeshift wooden theaters, for the first per-

exhilarating. And Roman etiquette permitted a guest to wrap up his or her *apophoreta*, or leftovers, in a napkin and take them home. On the negative side, a modern diner would find it awkward to recline on one side while eating, and both strange and messy to eat almost everything, no matter how slimy, with the hands (the main exception was soup or pudding, eaten with spoons).

Roman diners also engaged in some rather obnoxious habits. "Belching was considered a politeness," Carcopino points out, "justified by philosophers who thought the highest wisdom was to follow the dictates of nature."[91] Nature's dictates were taken to include farting, spitting, and even urinating in full view of the other guests. Martial described diners who snapped their fingers to summon slaves, who helped them relieve themselves into chamber pots without leaving the table. In order to prolong the enjoy-

In this modern engraving of a Roman street scene, people converse at one of the entrances to a stone theater. The mother and child have just been dropped off by the horse-drawn "taxi" at right.

manent stone theater, the Theater of Pompey, seating eight thousand, was not erected until 55 B.C. The city's two other stone theaters, named for Balbus and Marcellus, opened in 13 and 11 B.C., respectively. About 125 similar theaters appeared around the empire in the next two centuries. All featured a wide stage, the *pulpitum*, backed by a *scaenae frons*, or stage wall, on which scenery was painted or hung. Other typical features included roofs over the stages and curtains that were raised and lowered in front of them, awnings over the seating areas, vendors selling fast food and cushions, and showers to allow spectators to cool themselves on hot days when viewing many plays in succession.

Although theaters presenting formal written plays found an audience during the Empire, they took a backseat to other, more popular entertainments. Noteworthy among these were the mimes and pantomimes. The mimes were short, informal comic skits similar to the sketches on modern TV variety shows. Liversidge describes these skits as "scenes from everyday life with topical jokes and horseplay or disrespectful portrayals of the . . . gods, enlivened by dancing girls . . . jugglers and tightrope walkers."[94] Typical titles included "Wealthy Overnight," "The Pregnant Virgin," "Millionaire Goes Bankrupt," and "Love Locked Out."

The *fabula saltica*, or pantomimes, introduced in the early Empire, were balletlike presentations performed by a solo dancer, the *pantomimus*, who was accompanied by musicians and a choir singing a narration of the story the dance enacted. That the themes of pantomime were more serious and dignified than those of mime is reflected in its titles, which included "Chaos," "Cleopatra," and many named after Greek epics and tragedies. The second-century A.D. Greek writer Lucian praised the art of Roman pantomime, saying that "it sharpens the wits, it exercises the body, it delights the spectator, it instructs him in the history of bygone days, while eye and ear are held beneath the spell of flute and cymbal and of graceful dance."[95]

The Task of Amusing Rome

During the Empire, formal Roman plays often faced a sort of competition even stiffer than the mimes and pantomimes. In fact, theater audiences were known to walk out of a play in the middle of a performance on hearing that one of the public games, Rome's most popular form of entertainment by far, was about to begin. A thorough explanation of the origins of the various kinds of Roman games and the holidays on which they occurred would easily fill a volume of this size. Briefly stated, Rome's original public holidays were religious festivals known as *feriae*. Typically, celebrations consisted of prayer and sacrifice, followed by feasts and sometimes some small-scale sports contests. Larger contests and shows, the *ludi*, the most popular being the *ludi circenses*, or chariot races held in huge stadiums called circuses, began as the highlight of public celebrations after military victories; but over time these games came to be presented during the traditional *feriae*, too. Fights involving gladiators and wild animals, the *munera* shows, started out as part of the funeral ceremonies honoring members of the nobility. Private affairs at first, the *munera* became part of the public games in 44 B.C., shortly before Julius Caesar's assassination.

Shortly *after* Caesar's demise, as Augustus ushered in the Roman Empire, Rome's new rulers, the emperors, realized the potential of public entertainments for keeping the masses busy and content, and therefore less likely to protest or rebel. They also appeased "the mob" by providing periodic free distributions of grain to the poor.[96] According to Carcopino, Augustus and his successors

had in fact shouldered the dual task of feeding and amusing Rome. Their monthly [food] distributions . . . assured

The remains of the Theater of Marcellus, Rome's largest stone theater, built in 11 B.C. and named in honor of Augustus Caesar's beloved nephew.

This first-century A.D. terracotta plaque shows a quadrigarum, a four-horse chariot, speeding toward the turning posts at the end of the racetrack's spina. *The single horseman, partially visible at right, rides ahead, setting the race's frantic pace.*

the populace its daily bread. By the shows and spectacles . . . they occupied and disciplined [the mob's] leisure hours. . . . A people that yawns is ripe for revolt. The [emperors] saw to it that the Roman plebs suffered neither from hunger nor [boredom].[97]

This policy of appeasing the masses later became known as *panem et circenses*, or "bread and circuses," in reference to Juvenal's sarcastic remark in his tenth satire that the Roman mob "limits its anxious longings to two things only—bread, and the games of the circus!"[98]

Thousands Die as an Arena Collapses

Not all amphitheaters were sturdy stone buildings like the Colosseum. Some were makeshift wooden structures erected with little thought for safety, as evidenced by this excerpt from the Roman historian Tacitus's account (in his Annals) *of one that collapsed in the town of Fidenae in A.D. 27.*

"An ex-slave called Atilius started building an amphitheater at Fidenae for a gladiatorial show. But he neither rested its foundations on solid ground nor fastened the wooden superstructure securely. He had undertaken the project not because of great wealth or municipal ambition but for sordid profits. Lovers of such [gladiatorial] displays . . . flocked in—men and women of all ages. Their numbers, swollen by the town's proximity, intensified the tragedy. The packed structure collapsed, subsiding both inwards and outwards and . . . overwhelming a huge crowd of spectators and bystanders. Those killed at the outset of the catastrophe at least escaped torture. . . . More pitiable were those, mangled but not yet dead, who knew their wives and children lay there too. In daytime they could see them, and at night they heard their screams and moans. . . . When the ruins began to be cleared, people rushed to embrace and kiss the corpses—and even quarreled over them, when features were unrecognizable but similarities of physique or age had caused wrong identifications. Fifty thousand people were mutilated or crushed in the disaster."

This fine reconstruction of the Circus Maximus shows the long central axis, the spina, *dividing the racetrack, and the column-lined emperor's box rising in the stands at left.*

Apparently Juvenal exaggerated very little on this point. The chariot races held in the Circus Maximus were eagerly awaited and sold-out events at which huge masses of people jostled for seats or standing room. The Great Circus, begun in the early Republic and expanded and improved over the centuries, was, by the early second century A.D., one of the marvels of the world. It was some two thousand feet long and seven hundred feet wide and featured a long central axis, the *spina*, decorated with statues and obelisks, around which the chariots raced. Each of the twenty-four daily races was about five miles in length; although usually drawn by four horses, the chariots were sometimes hitched to teams of two, three, six, or even ten animals.

Winning drivers became national celebrities on a par with today's greatest auto racing, football, and basketball stars. Among the most famous were Flavius Scorpius, who

This sculptured relief depicts a winning athlete with his victory tokens—a laurel wreath and palm frond.

Bread and Circuses: Leisure Pursuits and Entertainments **73**

amassed 2,048 victories by the age of twenty-seven; Marcus Liber, with 3,000 wins; and Pompeius Muscosus, a winner 3,559 times. Some charioteers gained fame for their prowess in the *desultores*, special exhibitions in which the drivers performed wild acrobatics, such as jumping from one speeding chariot to another or climbing forward onto their galloping steeds.

In any event, the crowds applauded and loudly cheered the competitors from the stands. As at all Roman games, the spectators were a mix of men, women, freedmen, and slaves, for anyone who could find a place to sit or stand was admitted. Because they often watched for many hours at a stretch, spectators usually sat on cushions, either carried from home or rented at the stadium. They also periodically gorged themselves on fast food provided by roving vendors or *ther-mopolii* conveniently located beneath the stadium's walls. For those who desired other diversions, it was easy to find a *meretrix*, or female prostitute, or even a *saltatrix tonsa*, a cross-dressing male prostitute, both of whom roamed the circuses by the thousands during the games.

"We Who Are About to Die Salute You!"

The equally popular *munera* shows, including gladiator fights, fights between men and beasts or beasts and beasts, and mock land or naval battles, were usually staged in arenas called amphitheaters. The first stone arena in the empire was built in Pompeii between 70 and 65 B.C. and the first in Rome opened in 29 B.C. The latter remained the capital's only

Gladiators on Film

Unfortunately, few movie portrayals of ancient Roman gladiatorial combats have been accurately costumed or staged. Two of the exceptions were *Demetrius and the Gladiators* (1954, directed by Delmer Davies) and *Spartacus* (1960, directed by Stanley Kubrick). In *Demetrius*, the title character (played by Victor Mature) is a Greek freedman condemned to train at a gladiator school in Rome. At first, because he is a Christian, he refuses to fight. But when one of his friends dies at the hands of a gladiator, he changes his mind. Dressed as a *murmillo*, with helmet, greaves, and sword, he faces and defeats a *retiarius*, armed with net and trident, in an exhibition before the emperor Caligula, then goes on to defeat three other opponents simultaneously in a savage arena battle.

In *Spartacus*, the title character (played by Kirk Douglas) is the real-life slave who led a huge slave rebellion against the Roman state in the 70s B.C. Before escaping the gladiator school to which he was brought in chains, he is forced to fight a fellow student in a small arena to gratify a group of Roman notables who are visiting the school. Spartacus is arrayed as a "Thracian," with an exposed chest, small round shield, and short curved sword, while his opponent is a *retiarius*. Although the latter defeats Spartacus in the duel, he refuses to slay the fallen man and soon suffers death for his insolence. This scene, like the one in *Demetrius*, accurately re-creates the spectacle, excitement, and brutality of the Roman arena.

Gladiators fight to the death in a Roman arena. These warriors were the objects of a curious Roman double standard that on the one hand held them in disrepute as social outcasts, and on the other worshiped them as popular heroes embodying a special brand of honor.

permanent arena until A.D. 79, when the emperor Titus opened Rome's greatest and most famous example, the magnificent Colosseum.[99]

Modern experts estimate that over 3.5 million cubic feet of stone went into the Colosseum's construction. The beautifully decorated circular building was over 110 feet high and featured fifty-eight *vomitoria*, or entranceways, and an arena floor measuring 258 by 150 feet. The emperor and other notables sat in the *pulvinar*, or imperial box, which commanded the best view in the house. To keep the sun from baking the spectators on hot days, a huge *velarium*, or decorated awning, covered the structure's normally open top.[100]

On entering the arena, the gladiators, usually prisoners, slaves, criminals, or paid volunteers, first paraded around in a procession called a *pompa*. They were divided into various types of fighters; for example, a *retiarius* fought with a net and a long trident, but had no helmet or shield; a *murmillo* had both helmet and shield and brandished a sword. Men of different types were often paired off; and sometimes women fought against women, dwarves against dwarves, or women against dwarves. At the conclusion of the *pompa*, the combatants raised their weapons to the highest-ranking official present and recited the phrase *"Morituri te salutamus!"* or "We who are about to die salute you!" Then they fought, usually to the death. Seneca, who unlike most of his countrymen did not approve of these public slaughters, left behind this disquieting description:

> I've happened to drop in upon the midday entertainment of the arena in hope of . . . a touch of relief . . . [from the constant] glut of human blood. No, no: far from it. . . . Now for butchery pure and simple! The combatants have nothing to protect them: their bodies are utterly open to every blow: never a thrust but finds its mark. . . . What good is armor? What good is swordsmanship? All these things only put off death a little.[101]

The larger gladiatorial contests, which took place on special occasions, must have been particularly disturbing to people like Seneca. To celebrate a series of military successes, for instance, in A.D. 107 the emperor Trajan ordered more than ten thousand men into the arena within four months. And men were not the only victims. Animals, including bears, lions, panthers, deer, bulls, and

A gladiator fights a lion in one of the more exotic events featured in some munera *shows. There were also wild beast hunts in which men or women stalked wild animals and then slew them with arrows, spears, clubs, or other weapons.*

elephants, either mauled each other or met their ends at the points of Roman swords and spears. More than five thousand beasts were slaughtered in a single day when Titus inaugurated the Colosseum.

Modern historians are often highly critical of what they view as a depraved public bloodlust peculiar to the Romans. Carcopino, for example, writes, "The thousands of Romans who day after day . . . could take pleasure in this slaughter and not spare a tear . . . were learning nothing but contempt for human life and dignity."[102] And Henry Rowell makes this accusation: "The ugliest aspect of the gladiatorial and animal shows was its effect upon the audience. . . . [These displays were] inseparably connected with the excitement of bloodshed and death."[103] Yet, it should also be noted that the Romans viewed the gladiator as a model for a contemporary man of honor. Such a professional fighter was esteemed because he willingly submitted to the will of his masters, in this case the crowd of spectators who demanded he shed blood and if need be die for them. In this way, the gladiator's art represented less a contempt for human dignity and more a personification of that dignity. This was one way that the Romans' social attitudes, with their unusually strong emphasis on duty and subservience to higher authority, contrasted markedly with our own.

Supermarket of the World: Shipping, Trade, and Commerce

Throughout the Republic and the Empire, land and the life-supporting crops and livestock it produced remained the mainstay of the Mediterranean economy. Yet while farms and villages might achieve self-sufficiency, cities and armies could rarely be fed on what could be grown and raised locally. Large amounts of grain and other foodstuffs, as well as all manner of luxury goods, had to be imported, and that entailed shipping, trade, and commerce. The Romans quickly exploited this concept as they expanded outward from Italy and won dominion over the whole Mediterranean—*mare nostrum*, or "our sea," as they arrogantly came to call it. By the early Empire, a wide variety of foreign trade goods, along with the agricultural and mineral wealth of Greece, Palestine, Egypt, Spain, Gaul, and many other lands, flowed steadily along this marine highway and into the Roman heartland.

Indeed, that highway was the essential link that tied the Mediterranean world together, inducing all the major cities and cultural and trading centers to cluster along its shores. The territories stretching inland from the highly populated and developed coastlines were usually seen as secondary. As historian M. I. Finley puts it, they were lands "to be drawn upon for hides . . . metals and slaves, to be raided for booty . . . but to be inhabited by barbarians, not by Greeks or Romans."[104] The fourth-century B.C. Greek writer Plato had earlier expressed this reality, suggesting that "the earth is very vast, and . . . we who dwell in the [Mediterranean] region . . . inhabit a small portion only about the sea, like ants or frogs around a marsh."[105] The Romans took full advantage of this easy access to the civilized centers around the sea when their armies and navies subdued those who had built those centers. And that access continued to benefit Rome as its shipping and trading network spread its tendrils into every corner and niche of *mare nostrum's* shores.

A Huge Volume of Trade

The incredible breadth and diversity of the Roman trading network is well illustrated by a partial list of typical Italian imports: wheat from Egypt and northern Africa;[106] also from Africa, spices, wild animals for the public games, oil for lamps, and ivory and citrus wood for making and decorating fine furniture; from Spain and Gaul, copper pots and pans, pottery dishes, and fine wines; also from Spain, gold, silver, tin, and horses; from Syria, glass artifacts and fine textiles; from Britain, tin, lead, silver, cattle, and oysters; wool from the coasts of Asia Minor, linen from Egypt, and silk from faraway China; also from Egypt, papyrus to write on; from Athens, Greece, honey for sweetening foods;

from the Greek islands, fuller's earth, a mixture of clay and other minerals used for cleaning clothes; and from all parts of Greece, magnificent statues and paintings. Amazed to see such a rich variety of goods from so many far-flung provinces and countries come together in Rome, Aelius Aristides remarked, "If one would look at all these things, he must needs behold them either by visiting the entire civilized world or by coming to this city. . . . Here the merchant vessels come carrying these many products from all regions in every season . . . so that the city appears a kind of emporium [supermarket] of the world."[107]

The vast flow of goods into Italy was the largest but not the only aspect of Mediterranean commerce, for Italy exported products, too. According to Casson, the Romans

> sold abroad pottery and metalware and quantities of wine up to the end of the first century A.D. when [their] best cus-

tomers, the provinces, began not only to produce for themselves but to export to their former supplier. In the second century [Rome] partially made up for this loss: marble had then become the popular material for public buildings and she shipped out large amounts from the famous quarries at Carrara [in northwestern Italy].[108]

Not surprisingly, the huge and constant volume of imports and exports made a growing number of merchants and businessmen, many of them freedmen, rich. Some joined the ranks of the equestrian class, although many, despite their money, received the cold shoulder from older equestrian families and especially from patricians. Because most of Rome's upper-class wealth had originally come from land, most patricians looked down on trade and tradesmen. "Trade, if it is on a small scale," Cicero stated, "is to be considered vulgar." He went on to say that trade

Shoppers patronize a merchant's store on a busy Roman street. Note his signs painted, according to custom, directly on the building's outer wall.

This drawing depicts a Roman corn ship being loaded. Whenever possible, such vessels sailed within sight of land in order to avoid unexpected storms in the open sea.

was less vulgar on a larger scale, that is, if it produced a great deal of money. Tradesmen could redeem themselves entirely, he added, if they invested their newfound profits in the most respectable commodity—land. Trade, he said, "even seems to deserve high respect if those who are engaged in its pursuit . . . make their way from the port to a country estate." [109]

Considering this requirement for respectability, Cicero may well have approved of Tramalchio, the successful former slave of the first-century A.D. author Petronius and the main character in that writer's *Satyricon*. This excerpt, in which Tramalchio describes making his fortune and then buying a country house and cattle, captures the determination and enterprising spirit of many Roman merchants:

> I became crazy to go into business; and, not to bore you, I had five ships built, loaded them with wine (and wine at that time was worth its weight in gold), and sent them [from Asia Minor] to Rome. You'd imagine that it had been actually planned that way, for every blessed ship was wrecked, and that's fact and not fable. On one single day the sea swallowed down thirty million sesterces. Do you think I gave up? Not much! . . . I had

other ships built, bigger and better. . . . I loaded them with wine once more, with bacon, beans . . . and slaves. . . . In a single trip I piled up ten million sesterces. . . . I built me a house and bought all the cattle that were offered for sale. . . . [Later] I retired from business and began to lend money to freedmen. [110]

Merchant Shipping

The cargo ships that carried goods for merchants like Tramalchio were wooden sailing vessels. The hulls were covered with pitch, an oily petroleum residue, to keep them watertight, and painted with a mixture of soft wax and colored pigments. Judging from the remains of wrecks recently excavated from the sea bottom, most of these ships were about 60 to 100 feet long and 17 to 30 feet wide and carried cargoes ranging from 50 to 250 tons.

A few cargo ships, notably those that ferried grain from Egypt to Rome for distribution to the mob or that lugged heavy stone artifacts, were much larger. In A.D. 40, the emperor Caligula had a stone obelisk (which now stands outside St. Peter's Basilica in the Vatican) shipped to the capital from Egypt.

Pompey and the Pirates

Pirates were a common threat to merchant shipping through most of Rome's early centuries, one that grew particularly dangerous in the early first century B.C. In one of the most daring and successful military operations of all times, the renowned general Gnaeus Pompey eliminated that threat, as described here by Lionel Casson in The Ancient Mariners.

"In 67 B.C. when the pirate menace had become a national crisis, the people of Rome handed Pompey a blank check to cope with it. The whole shore line of the Mediterranean up to a point fifty miles

inland, with all the resources therein, was turned over to him; he had the authority to requisition ships or men or money or whatever else he needed from any governor of any Roman province or from any king bound by allegiance to Rome. . . . The key to Pompey's success was . . . the scale and thoroughness of his planning: his strategy left nothing to chance and it embraced the whole of the Mediterranean. He divided the shore line into thirteen sectors each with its own commander and fleet. . . . Each fleet was to attack the pirate nests in its sector simultaneously while Pompey, at the head of a mobile force of sixty vessels, swept from Gibraltar eastward, driving all before him. . . . It was a spectacular operation, brilliantly conceived and magnificently executed. In three months Pompey had [swept the sea clean of pirates, accomplishing] what no power had been able to do for centuries. Except for a spasmodic outburst now or then, the age-old plague of the Mediterranean was ended for a long time to come."

Gnaeus Pompey, one of the Roman Republic's greatest military heroes, distinguished himself fighting pirates, rebellious slaves, and other enemies of the state.

The boat that transported it was specially built to carry a burden of thirteen hundred tons. When a big grain galley strayed off course and ended up at Athens's port of Piraeus in the second century A.D., Lucian examined it and penned this description:

What a size the ship was! One-hundred and eighty feet in length, the ship's carpenter told me . . . and 44 feet from the deck to the lowest point in the hold. . . . The crew was like an army. They told me she carried enough grain to feed every mouth in Athens for a year. And it all depends for its safety on one little old man who turns those great steering oars with a tiller that's no more than a stick! They pointed him out to me; wool-haired little fellow, half-bald; Heron was his name, I think.[111]

Heron and other merchant captains had no instruments to guide them. For navigation they relied on special nautical books that advised the best routes and sailing times, and particularly on observations of the sun, moon, and stars. Also aiding them were many coastal lighthouses that employed polished metal plates to reflect light generated by bonfires.

Merchants and sailors were often away from home for weeks or months at a time. While docking at ports, they stayed in *tabernae*, small inns with colorful names like "The Wheel," "The Elephant," and "The Rooster," which featured hard, uncomfortable beds but affordable prices. Merchants who traveled inland to and among the cities often stayed at guest houses called *mansiones*, which were

located every fifteen miles or so along all main roads. Fortunately for these tradesmen, by the end of the first century A.D. the extensive system of fine paved roads that covered Italy and the populated sections of the provinces facilitated easy transport of goods from one city to another.

Craftsmen and Guilds

The merchants who utilized the roadways carried not only foreign goods but also goods produced by native and local industries. For example, winemaking was one of the most important Italian industries. Native vineyards produced more than fifty kinds of famous wines, of which the capital city alone consumed some 25 million gallons per year, enough to supply every man, woman, and child, slave or free, with two quarts a week. Other widespread Italian industries included olive oil production, leather tanning, marble quarrying, pottery making, and metalworking, which produced artifacts of gold, silver, bronze, iron, and copper. Furniture making

The expert craftsmanship of Roman metalworkers is well illustrated in the elegant design and elaborate detail of this set of silver dinnerware.

(Right) In a cloth-making factory, two workers examine a bolt of fabric; (below) a woman pharmacist is shown with some of the tools of her trade. A number of Roman women, many of them widows, practiced trades and/or owned or operated businesses.

by *fabri lignarii*, or woodworkers, and *citrarii*, or cabinetmakers, was also an important industry. Various towns and regions were known for a particular craft or product and depended on shipping to satisfy widespread demand.

The workers of the various trades and industries often banded together in local guilds and trade associations, known as *collegia*, or colleges. These were not trade unions or mutual aid societies; nor did they train apprentices as did the guilds that developed later in medieval times. Veyne explains:

In principle, the *collegia* were free, private associations, whose members were free men and slaves who practiced a common trade or worshipped a common god. Nearly every city boasted one or more. In one town, for example, there was a weavers' association and a college of worshippers of Hercules. . . . Members lived in the town and knew one another. All were men; no women were admitted.[112]

Evidently, the Roman workers' colleges were essentially clubs that afforded low-income men the opportunity to meet and socialize away from the company of women. The clubs charged dues, which were used to pay for members-only banquets and also to provide needy members with funerals. Slaves often joined the *collegia* to make sure they would receive a decent burial after they died.

Money and Banking

The members of the *collegia*, along with all the other craftsmen, merchants, and tradesmen in Rome's vast system of foreign and domestic commerce, depended for their livelihoods on a stable currency. The Mediterranean market was extremely widespread and diverse, encompassing dozens of different peoples, languages, and native monetary systems. To make trade simple and reliable, and thereby to keep its economy strong and viable, Rome maintained a currency made up of coins that were recognized, accepted, and of standard value all over its empire.[113]

During the prosperous *Pax Romana* of the early Empire, the most common coins, ranging from most to least valuable, were: the *aureus*, made of about a quarter ounce of gold; the silver *denarius* (plural, *denarii*), worth $1/25$ of an *aureus*; the bronze *sesterce*, or *sestertius*, equal to $1/4$ of a *denarius* (or $1/100$ of an *aureus*); the copper *as*, worth $1/4$ of a *sestertius*; and the copper *quadrans*, valued at $1/4$ of an *as* (or $1/1600$ of an *aureus*). Modern equivalent values for these coins are difficult to determine. But some idea of their buying power can be deduced by the fact that the fee for a boy or girl to attend elementary school in the early first century A.D. was about 8 *asses* (or 2 *sesterces*) a month. In that same era a teacher earned probably 15 to 20 *denarii* a month, a soldier about 18 to 25 *denarii*, and an average worker with a small family to support perhaps 20 to 40 *denarii*.

Classes of Roman Workers

Roman workers, craftsmen, and traders were roughly divided into three groups. The first consisted of poor plebs who owned no share of the businesses in which they labored and were fortunate if they could eke out simple livings from day to day. They ranged from farm laborers to construction workers to messengers and porters. The second group was made up of poor shopkeepers and craftsmen, such as snack bar operators and cobblers, who ran their own businesses but lacked enough cash to invest in large amounts or wide varieties of stock. They had to get up early each morning to buy the goods they hoped to sell that day. The fact that they could buy and transport only a modest amount of goods on any one day severely limited the amount of money they could make on that day. The members of the third group of workers were generally well-to-do individuals who owned property and many slaves, and who sold goods to both the public and the small shopkeepers. This wealthiest group included shippers like Tramalchio, bakers who owned and operated grain mills as well as ovens and shops, and butchers who could afford to buy whole herds of cattle and dozens or even hundreds of slaves to tend and slaughter them.

This example of a gold aureus, *the most valuable of Roman coins, bears the image of Domitia, wife of the first-century* A.D. *emperor Domitian.*

Banks and bankers were as integral to Rome's economy as the coins themselves. In most cases, Roman bankers, called *argentarii*, were private businessmen, most of them equestrians or freedmen, as patricians generally considered dealing with money to be beneath their dignity. The *argentarii* provided a number of essential services. According to noted historian Will Durant, "They served as money-changers, accepted checking accounts and interest-bearing deposits . . . managed, bought, and sold realty [land and buildings], placed investments and collected debts, and lent money to individuals and partnerships."[114] When the wealthy freedman Tramalchio began lending money to freedmen of lesser means, he became an *argentarius*. Agents for these bankers typically ran *mensa publica*, or money-changing tables, in forums, marketplaces, and other central public areas. Along with the farmers, shippers, traders, merchants, and craftsmen, the bankers helped to maintain the ceaseless flow of goods that was vital to Rome's economy and to the everyday sustenance, comforts, and well-being of its people.

CHAPTER 8

Diverse Paths to Heavenly Truths: Roman Religious Beliefs

"We have overcome all the nations of the world," wrote Cicero in the last years of the Republic, "because we have realized that the world is directed and governed by the gods."[115] He specifically meant the Roman gods, of course. Like other master politicians, Cicero regularly invoked the gods, whether he personally believed in them or not, to justify one state policy or another.

This approach was not new. From the beginning, Rome's leaders had taken full advantage of the Roman people's deep religious faith and ready acceptance of a wide array of superstitions involving gods, spirits, and fate. Religious beliefs supported state policy and vice versa. On the one hand, as the Romans came to see themselves and their system as superior and were successful in their conquests, it became natural to attribute that success to fate or the will of the gods. On the other hand, the belief that the gods favored their nation above all others fed the Romans' arrogant conviction that they had a destiny to rule the world.

While religious beliefs helped to shape state policy and motivated the Romans as a people, they also provided guidance and comfort for the individual in his or her everyday life. The relationship that developed between a person and the gods took the form of a sacred contract. "If man observed all the proper ritual in his worship," writes historian Arthur E. R. Boak, "the god was bound to act [favorably]. . . . If man failed in his duty, the god punished him."[116] The Latin expression coined to describe this contractual relationship was *do ut des*, meaning "I, the mortal, give to you, the god, so that you may give back to me." Thus, the various beliefs and rituals of Roman religion kept two important relationships bound securely—the first a kind of political alliance between the gods and the state, and the second a contract for mutual appeasement between the gods and the individual.

Spirits and Gods

The Romans had attempted to maintain a good working relationship with the spiritual world since their dimly remembered tribal days. The earliest Romans worshiped spirits they thought resided in everything around them, including inanimate objects like rocks and trees, a belief system now called animism. Some of these minor deities, the *numina*, regularly watched over and presumably even directed many aspects of people's daily lives. "Every activity of country life," Mattingly explains, "every act in [a] trade or profession, every expression of personal life may be considered to be under the ward of its own little god. There is a god to teach you how to plow and . . . a god to teach the infant how to suck and how to walk, and so on; there are gods of nurture and gods of marriage."[117]

The Romans usually divided the *numina* into convenient groups. Household spirits included the *penates*, who protected the family food storage; the *lares*, who kept the home safe and also guarded streets and crossroads; and the *manes*, spirits of deceased ancestors, who watched over various family members. The Romans also recognized a special type of guardian spirit known as the *genius*. They believed that each family was protected by its unique *genius*, who inhabited the body of the living paterfamilias and secured the continuity of the family line by passing from father to son on the father's death. The materfamilias's *genius*, who passed from her body to that of her daughter, was called the Juno. These guardian spirits, comments Mattingly, were, "in a sense, the life of the race."[118]

At first, the Romans pictured the various spirits as natural forces rather than as formal deities. In time, however, some spirits did

Roman worshipers sacrifice to Jupiter. In most ancient societies, sacrifice and prayer were the two principal religious rituals.

begin to take on human appearance and personalities. These became gods and goddesses, such as Vesta, goddess of the hearth; Janus, who watched over the doorway; and Mars, protector of farmers' fields.

Over the centuries, as they came into contact with peoples more cultured than themselves, the highly impressionable and adaptive Romans incorporated foreign religious concepts and gods, particularly those of the Etruscans and Greeks, into their own faith. Thus, the Etruscan sky god, Jupiter, and the Greek head god, Zeus, merged into the Roman supreme god, Jupiter. And the Roman field protector, Mars, became associated with and eventually assumed the same identity as Ares, the Greek god of war. Other important Roman gods that developed in Rome's early centuries were Juno, Jupiter's wife and protector of women and childbirth; Neptune, ruler of the sea; Venus, goddess of beauty and love; Minerva, goddess of war and protector of craftsmen; Mercury, Jupiter's messenger, who protected travelers and tradesmen; and Apollo, the versatile deity of the sun, music, healing, and prophecy.

Perceptions of and ways of worshiping these gods naturally evolved and changed over time. However, all through the Republic and the Empire the most powerful and revered of what came to be considered the traditional Roman deities remained the members of the so-called Capitoline Triad. All originally Etruscan gods, these were Jupiter, his symbols the eagle (which the Romans adopted as their own symbol) and the thunderbolt; Juno, her symbol the peacock; and Minerva, her symbol the owl. Their collective name referred to the Capitoline hill in Rome on which their temple, the Capitolium, loomed perpetually above and, many people believed, protected the Eternal City.[119]

How to Outwit the Heavens

The Romans did not distinguish religion from superstition and almost everyone, from the least to most educated, believed strongly in astrology, the belief system that claims that the heavenly bodies have a direct and controlling influence on the lives of human beings. In this excerpt from The World of Rome, *Michael Grant defines this belief and explains how it coexisted with those involving formal deities.*

"The specific features of different cults and gods were ever intermingled with one another. This 'syncretism' [fusion of diverse belief systems] presents a weird, unceasing series of attempts to define and explain the true nature of the godhead [divine being or beings]—who directed . . . the eternal and majestic movement of the heavenly bodies which controlled human lives. . . . These heavenly bodies . . . and particularly the seven planets [in ancient times thought to comprise Mercury, Venus, Mars, Jupiter, Saturn, the sun, and the moon] and twelve signs of the zodiac, were believed . . . to be the controllers of the human race. It was also felt . . . that if one possessed the necessary knowledge their decrees could be read and discovered beforehand. . . . One of the principal activities of the professional astrologer was to cast horoscopes. . . . The theory of this was that the . . . astrologers, by finding out the days, hours, and minutes [when planetary influences were strongest or weakest], could advise their clients how to outwit the heavens by planning or avoiding undertakings at appropriate times and seasons."

Meanwhile, even as highly complex and formal cults and rituals developed around these deities, most Romans continued to worship many of their *numina*, including household spirits like the *lares*. Writing in the early Empire, Juvenal called on his personal spirits to tell him how he might avoid dying a pauper: "O my own little Lares, whom I . . . pray to by offering a pinch of frankincense [a spice] or spelt [a kind of wheat], or with a tiny garland, when can I assure myself of what will keep my old days from the beggar's staff?"[120]

Sacrifice and Prayer

By praying to his spirits and offering them tokens of appeasement, Juvenal performed the two main rituals that fulfilled the unwritten spiritual contract between the gods and humans. Besides offering up certain plants or personal items, people often appeased the gods by sacrificing animals such as oxen, goats, sheep, and pigs. Usually, someone led the victim of an intended sacrifice to an altar in front of a temple dedicated to the god who was to be appeased. Sacrifice and other public or group ceremonies did not take place inside the temple, which was generally reserved for quiet contemplation and prayer by individual priests or lay worshipers. After sprinkling salt, flour, or wine over the beast's head, a priest slit its throat, cut it up, and then threw parts of its body into the altar fire for the god to consume. It was important to get all the steps of the ritual right, for if a single detail was wrong the god, it was believed, would refuse the sacrifice.

The use of strict formulas was also important in the other major ritual, prayer. According to Liversidge, "The object of prayer was

On the eve of a military campaign, a Roman general performs an elaborate sacrifice to ensure that the gods will favor the venture.

to attract a god's attention and the success of a worshiper's request depended upon the use of correct forms. . . . If mistakes were made the prayer would be useless and have to be repeated correctly."[121] Thus, a person learned to begin one kind of prayer with the exact wording, "I beg, pray, and beseech you," and other kinds of prayers with different phrases.

As to the content of prayers, the Romans prayed for many of the same things people pray for today. The first-century A.D. humorist Persius made the point that when praying aloud in front of others people usually asked for socially acceptable things such as "a sound mind" or "good credit." In private, however, a man might mutter: "O if only my uncle would pop off!" or "If only Hercules [god of unexpected gain] would [send me] a crock of silver!" or "If only I could wipe out that ward of mine who stands next before me in the [family] succession."[122] Juvenal offered this penetrating and moving observation whose truths apply in all ages:

> Few people in the world know what constitutes real happiness. Most pray for blessings that bring about their ruin. The usual ambitions are eloquence, physical strength, wealth, political power, military glory, beauty. . . . Wealth causes many to be strangled or poisoned. . . . Political power causes envy and headlong ruin. . . . Many pray for a long life. But old age is filled with unhappiness of all kinds—physical ugliness . . . deafness . . . paralysis, senility, the deaths of all one's rela-

tives. . . . What is there left to pray for in order to achieve happiness? A sound mind in a sound body; courage not to fear death; ability to endure hardship; and, above all, virtue.[123]

Alternative Religions

The traditional gods and spirits were not the only deities the Romans worshiped. As their empire expanded in the late Republic and

Of Virtues and Angels

Still another Roman belief system that coexisted right alongside the traditional religion, the imported cults, and astrology, was what is best described as "virtue worship." The Romans (and many other ancients) held that certain concepts, such as justice, truth, virtue, and success, were manifested in and directed by special deities. These spirits, including, among others, Justice, Beauty, Concord, Truth, Success, Health, and Victory, were seen, like the major gods, as having human form, as possessing specific, recognizable functions and powers, and as capable of receiving worship. Accordingly, the goddess Concord and her fellow virtue-deities received the regular prayers of millions of Romans all through the Republic and Empire. The worship of Victory was especially fervent, for she was seen as a guiding force behind the many military and political successes of the long-lived Roman state.

Toward the end of the Empire, the Christians condemned such worship as just another aspect of "corrupt" paganism. In A.D. 383, under pressure from religious leaders, the emperor Gratian removed Victory's public altar, which had stood in Rome's Senate House for many generations, an act that many non-Christian Romans protested to no avail. Yet, while the Christians tried to eradicate pagan virtue worship, they steadily incorporated the idea into their own faith in the form of angels. Thus, the Roman virtue Clemency survived as the Christian angel called Mercy, and the Roman spirit Victory, her ancient altar banished, became the angel of Victory, her original form—including wings, victor's wreath, and palm—remaining almost unchanged in the transition.

A statuette of Tyche, goddess of fortune, one of the principal minor deities involved in virtue worship.

This carving of the hero/god Mithras slaying a bull now rests in Boston's Museum of Fine Arts. Mithras was just one of many foreign deities Rome imported in the late Republic and early Empire.

early Empire, they came into contact with and adopted many foreign gods, whose cults spread to Italy and grew into viable alternatives to the traditional state religion. Among the most popular of the imported gods were

Cybele, known as the Great Mother, introduced from Asia Minor, a nature and fertility deity whose priests castrated themselves to appease her; Isis, an Egyptian goddess whom the Romans associated with goodness and

"Leaping About Like Maniacs"

One of the most bizarre of the eastern cults that filtered into Rome was that of the Syrian goddess, Atargatis, pictured by her followers as half-human and half-fish, whose priests were all eunuchs, or castrated men. The second-century A.D. *Roman writer Apuleius was so fascinated and amused by the antics of these priests that he recorded them in his work,* The Golden Ass, *a humorous tale about a man who is accidentally transformed into an ass, experiences colorful adventures, and is finally restored to human form by the goddess Isis. Apuleius's detailed description of Atargatis's devoted followers reads, in part:*

"The eunuch priests prepared to go out on their rounds, all dressed in different colors

and looking absolutely hideous, their faces dabbed with rouge and their eyesockets painted to bring out the brightness of their eyes. . . . They covered the Goddess with a silk mantle [cloth] and . . . they started brandishing enormous swords and maces [clubs], leaping about like maniacs. . . . Every now and then they would bite themselves savagely and as a climax cut their arms with the sharp knives that they carried. One of them let himself go . . . more than the rest. . . . He began making a bogus confession of guilt, crying out . . . that he had in some way offended against the holy laws of his religion. Then he [used] his own hands to inflict the necessary punishment and snatching up [a whip] . . . gave himself a terrific flogging."

purification of sin; and from Persia and India, Mithras, whose followers professed that all people, regardless of wealth or social position, were equally worthy and deserved to be treated with kindness and respect.

The fact that the Romans readily embraced so many alternative religions shows how uniquely tolerant they were of others' faiths. To an average Roman, worshiping a certain preferred god or gods did not suggest that all other gods in the world were false or inferior. Most people matter-of-factly accepted the idea that there were many diverse paths to the same heavenly truths.

The common misconception that the Romans were religiously intolerant stems from their harsh treatment of the members of another cult that spread to Rome from the east. These were the early Christians, so often depicted in modern novels and films being burned at the stake, crucified, or thrown to the lions in the arena. But these persecutions stemmed largely from the Christians' apparent antisocial attitudes, including their own marked religious intolerance, rather than from their adherence to an alternative belief system. "The Christians," Mattingly comments,

In this painting by the nineteenth-century French artist Jean Gerome, Christian martyrs face a cruel death in the crowded Circus Maximus.

Funerals and Burials

Roman funeral and burial practices varied considerably. Poor people were usually cremated, although some well-to-do persons also chose this method. In a simple cremation, mourners dug a pit, placed the body in it along with some dry wood, and set it ablaze. A more elaborate and expensive version involved a ceremonial pyre, a raised wooden platform, on which relatives placed the body and some of the deceased's clothes and belongings. After cremation, the ashes were collected and placed in urns. Many families kept such urns in their homes, while others chose to store them in underground vaults called *columbarii*, which they periodically visited to pay their respects.

Of those who chose (or had chosen for them) burial, the vast majority of urban poor ended up in mass graves, the sites of which were often forgotten over time. Those who could afford it rested in coffins called sarcophagi. Mourners marched in a solemn procession through the city streets, carrying the body on a litter and stopping at least once, usually in the Forum, for a funeral oration. The procession then proceeded outside the city, where the mourners placed the body in a stone or marble sarcophagus, often ornately decorated and sometimes bearing a carved likeness of the deceased. Such coffins rested in stone tombs or under elaborately carved tombstones, both of which commonly lined the roadsides outside the cities, giving the impression of rows of miniature buildings.

refused to worship the gods, insisting on the supremacy of one God of their own. . . . They were inclined to abstain from the good things of life—from theaters, banquets, shows of amphitheater and circus. More than this, they were suspected [mistakenly] of horrible crimes—child murder, incest—and of a hatred for the whole human race.[124]

Despite continued periodic persecutions, however, the Christians persevered and over the centuries grew in number and influence. In the early fourth century A.D. the emperor Constantine converted to the faith, which a few decades later became Rome's official religion. That Christianity remained dogmatic and intolerant can be inferred from the fact that when it achieved this official status the traditional Roman religion, along with all other faiths, was discouraged and eventually banned.

"I Conquer Death"

One aspect of Christianity that appealed very much to many Romans, especially the poor and downtrodden, a belief that contributed significantly to its steady growth during the Empire, was its promise of eternal life in heaven. The traditional state religion originally also included belief in an afterlife. Following ideas borrowed from the Greeks, most early Romans thought that when a person died his or her spirit crossed over the mystical River Styx to Hades, or the "underworld." This nether region was divided into Elysium, where good souls went, and Tartarus, where sinners suffered eternal torments. But over time many people lost faith in this and other concepts of the traditional religion. By the early Empire, large numbers of people believed that death was final and that nothing awaited human souls, be they good or bad, but the dark stillness of the grave. "After death nothing is," wrote Seneca. "Dead, we become the lumber of the world. . . . Hell and the foul fiend that rules [it] . . . are senseless stories, idle tales, dreams, whimsies, and no more."[125] Inscriptions on tombstones regularly echoed this same theme. "I believe in nothing beyond the grave," reads one. "There is no Hades," asserts another.[126] Juvenal summed up the general mood of his time, recording that while some people still feared and worshiped the gods, plenty of others "believe that the world has no governor to move it."[127]

One of Christianity's most important feats was to restore for new generations of Romans the hope that such a divine governor did indeed exist and that the faithful would achieve eternal salvation. It was not alone in this promise. The cult of Isis, for instance, also promised eternal life, which explains why it remained popular for so long. "I conquer Fate and Fate obeys me,"[128] was that goddess's clarion call. But for a variety of reasons, some of which remain unexplained, more Romans ended up answering Christianity's call. It was, after all, Christ's doctrine, and not that of Isis, that captured the hearts of Constantine and a majority of latter-day Romans and, after managing to survive Rome's demise, spread to the far reaches of the globe.

Marching the Paths of Glory: Life in the Roman Army

In the centuries of conquest that brought them a vast empire, the Romans established a unique, complex, and very proud military tradition and became masters of the art of warfare. The traditions and actions of the Roman army "exercised profoundly far-reaching effects on all subsequent history," remarks Michael Grant. "For this was one of the greatest and most formidable armies that has ever existed." Because so many men served in Rome's army and navy, especially during its many wars, military service and all the political and social customs that supported it had a significant impact on Roman life. And in turn, Grant points out, that impact was transmitted to later cultures: "It was the conditions the Roman army created which enabled Rome to bring . . . its vast, pecu-

liar . . . contributions to civilization, which have to such a large extent made our modern life, for better or worse, what it is."[129]

Attitudes About the Military

Romans of all walks of life accepted and supported the concept of a strong military, for offensive as well as defensive purposes. Today, while most people concede the need to maintain armies for defense, civilized nations rarely amass military forces specifically for the aim of conquest. By contrast, the Romans, like most other ancient peoples, thought it perfectly natural for the strong to impose their will on the weak. And because they sincerely believed that their own race

This marble relief from Praeneste (now Palestrina), near Rome, shows a Roman warship. The Egyptian crocodile emblem on the lower prow suggests that this was one of the vessels commanded by Mark Antony, who had teamed up with Egypt's queen, Cleopatra VII, in a civil war against the Roman state.

and ideas were superior and also that they had a destiny to rule others, Romans saw it almost as their moral obligation to spread those ideas and fulfill that destiny.

Consequently, most Romans were fiercely proud and supportive of the army, navy, and soldiering in general. For many young Roman men, military service, especially glory on the battlefield, helped to make names, shape careers, and distinguish entire families. Such pride and grand aspirations infected not only Italian-born citizens, but also many young men of the provinces, who were eager to become a part of the elite forces that had subdued the known world and at the same time to prove themselves real and good Romans. In a surviving letter, a second-century A.D. Egyptian boy named Apion enthusiastically wrote to his father about his experiences in the Roman navy. "When I arrived at Misenum [the port where his fleet was docked] I received from the government three gold pieces for my traveling expenses," he proudly boasted. Following the custom of foreign-born soldiers and sailors, with equal pride he changed his name to a "good" Roman one: "My [new] name is Antonius Maximus, my ship the *Athenonice*. Good-bye."[130]

A few rebellious individuals did not buy into Rome's famed military ethic. More contemptuous of soldiering, of mighty generals leading thousands to their deaths, and of the often tragic ends those leaders met, Juvenal wrote boldly:

> Many prize military glory above all. Hannibal brought ruin to his native Carthage by his vast military ambitions, and suicide for himself. Death overtook the mighty conqueror Alexander the Great, and King Xerxes of the Persians. The paths of glory lead but to the grave.[131]

Once they became part of the military establishment, Juvenal contended, many decent men turned arrogant and mean and took advantage of their positions by bullying civilians. One of the many benefits of soldiering, he said, is "that no civilian will dare to thrash you; if thrashed himself, he must hold his tongue, and not venture to exhibit . . . the teeth that have been knocked out, or the black and blue lumps upon his face." Trying to prosecute the bully was useless, insisted Juvenal, for most people were inclined to back the military no matter what. "Sooner you will find a false witness against a civilian than one who will tell the truth against the honor of a soldier."[132]

How the Army Developed

Juvenal and his opinions were in the minority; many more thousands of young men eagerly sought the honor and other benefits of military service. Of course, the army of Juvenal's day was considerably different from the ones that had marched outward from the Latium plain when Rome was still a jumble of rude farmers' shacks. In the early Republic, soldiers were a very elite group, mainly landowners of Italian birth, and also mostly citizen militia, who entered the service when the government called on them during an emergency and then returned to their farms when the fighting ended. Later, as military campaigns grew longer and took the troops farther from home, the government began paying the soldiers, some of whom (mainly officers) became career professionals. This early army consisted of large battalions called legions, each having about 4,200 men, with smaller subdivisions of 100 men each, called centuries. When arrayed on the battlefield, the legions broke down into fighting units called maniples, most containing about 120 men.

The more formidable and efficient army that emerged in the last century of the Republic resulted largely from the reforms of the famous general Gaius Marius. He removed the rule that soldiers had to own property, thus opening up military service to many plebs and other lower-class Romans who otherwise would have been unemployed. Marius also increased pay, made training more rigorous, and standardized both training and weapons. These incentives notwithstanding, the majority of tough, skilled fighters who became known as "Marius's mules" remained irregulars who signed on for campaigns of set duration and departed with a hefty bonus at their conclusions. Soon after Marius, Julius Caesar and other leaders began supplementing these core forces by recruiting *auxilia*, noncitizens from the provinces. "At the outset they fought in their native fashion with their native weapons," Casson writes, "but as time went on, they were more and more assimilated to the legions' way of fighting. On discharge they were granted citizenship."[133]

In this later republican army most legions had five to six thousand men, divided into centuries of eighty rather than a hundred men each. Each century broke down further into ten *contubernia*. Made up of eight men who shared the same tent and traveled and ate together, the *contubernium* was the equivalent of the modern army platoon or squad. The maniple had been replaced by an even more flexible battlefield unit called the cohort, usually consisting of about five hundred men (special cohorts had about eight hundred), which could move quickly as a detached unit or combine with other cohorts.

The Whole Army Is but One Body

This excerpt from The Wars of the Jews *by the ancient Jewish historian Flavius Josephus illustrates how the skill, efficiency, and discipline of the Roman army commanded widespread admiration and respect, even among peoples whom that army had once conquered.*

"[Any person] will be forced to confess that [the Romans'] obtaining so large a dominion has been the acquisition of their valor, and not the bare gift of fortune. . . . When they are to fight, they leave nothing without planning, nor to be done off-hand, but counsel is ever first taken before any work is begun, and what has been there resolved upon is put into execution presently; for which reason they seldom commit any errors; and if they have been mistaken at any time, they easily correct those mistakes. . . . And as to what melancholy accidents happen unexpectedly, there is this comfort in them, that they [the Romans] had however taken the best consultations [precautions] they could to prevent them. . . . When they come to a battle, the whole army is but one body, so well coupled together are their ranks, so sudden are their movements, so sharp their hearing as to what orders are given them . . . and so nimble are their hands when they set to work; whereby it comes to pass that what they do is done quickly, and what they suffer they bear with the greatest patience . . . what wonder is it that [they have won so great an empire]? One might well say that the Roman possessions are not inferior to the Romans themselves."

A Soldier's Life

Without the incentive of this generous pension, maintaining an effective standing army would have been very difficult, for the regular pay was low and a soldier's life was usually difficult, monotonous, and dangerous. Typically, a young man in his late teens or early twenties who wanted to enlist reported to his nearest recruiting station, just as prospective professional soldiers do today. He was expected to produce documents proving he was either a citizen and therefore eligible for the legions, or a provincial who would be assigned to the *auxilia* (this rule was dropped, of course, after the A.D. 212 edict making provincials citizens). If he met the height requirement of five feet eight inches, he received a physical exam and, assuming he passed, took the oath of service and headed for boot camp. According to Casson, in basic training a recruit

Gaius Marius, Julius Caesar's uncle, instituted sweeping reforms in army structure and discipline.

During the Empire, Augustus Caesar established more permanent standing forces of career professionals, with standard hitches of twenty-five years for the army and twenty-six for the navy. The yearly salary for regular soldiers in the first century A.D. was 225 *denarii* (raised to 300 in the following century), from which they had to pay for their own clothing and rations. Low-ranking officers got about double that amount and all soldiers received a bonus of 3,000 *denarii*, about thirteen years pay, as a pension when they finished their hitches.[134]

ran and jumped to harden his physique, learned to swim, practiced marching with the standard military pace, which enabled troops to cover twenty-four miles in five hours, and took lessons in handling the legionary's standard weapon, the short sword; at the outset he hacked with a wooden sword at a wooden stake, a technique introduced into the army from the gladiator schools.[135]

The recruit also trained with other offensive weapons, especially a javelin, or throwing spear, called a *pilum*, which featured a point strategically fashioned of soft metal. "If the enemy stopped the missile with his shield," Grant explains in *The Army of the Caesars*, "it stuck there at an angle and he could neither go on using his shield nor throw the javelin back, because it was bent and buckled. And if

The details of Roman army uniforms and weapons, including the pilum, *or throwing spear, are plainly visible in this raised bas-relief.*

overhead for protection from enemy rocks, arrows, and spears. Lastly, the recruit was trained in the rapid making and breaking of an elaborate camp that included a sturdy stockade, a process the Romans developed practically into an art form. The first-century A.D. Jewish historian Flavius Josephus, who greatly admired the discipline of the Roman army, described such a camp in his *Wars of the Jews*:

> The outward circumference [of the camp] resembles a wall, and is adorned with towers at equal distances, where between the towers stand the devices for throwing arrows and darts, and for slinging stones. . . . They also erect four gates . . . wide enough for making excursions, if occasion should require. They divide the camp . . . into two streets . . . and place the tents of the commanders in the middle. . . . It appears to be a [miniature] city built suddenly, with its marketplace, and a place for handicraft trades [and so on]. . . . When they have thus secured themselves, they live together . . . with quietness and decency, as are all their other affairs managed with good order and security.[137]

the javelin missed the enemy's body and shield alike and fell to the ground, the result was the same . . . it could not be thrown back."[136]

Once the recruit was in shape and had completed his initial weapons training, he had to get used to marching with a full pack, consisting of some sixty pounds of weapons, tools, and rations. Then he learned about the standard battlefield moves, in which one or more cohorts formed various lines, wedges, and circles for either offensive or defensive purposes. He also learned how to create a *testudo*, or turtle, a squared, tightly packed formation of men all holding their shields

Once a full-fledged soldier, and providing that he lived long enough, an ambitious and hardworking young man had the chance to move up in the ranks. The first step was to become a clerk or orderly to a high-ranking officer, a duty that brought no extra pay but did exempt one from hard work details such as erecting the stockade, digging ditches, or building bridges over streams. Next, the soldier might become a *signifer*, roughly a corporal in rank, who bore his century's standards while marching or in battle. A more prestigious job was that of *aquilifer*, who bore

Roman War Fleets

Rome's first war fleets, built during the First Punic War (264–241 B.C.) to meet the threat of Carthage's formidable navy, consisted of quinqueremes, vessels with either five banks of oars or five rowers to an oar. After Rome defeated Carthage in this war, in which warships played the decisive role, few important naval battles occurred during the remainder of the Republic and Empire, mainly because war fleets tended to be used as secondary or supplementary supports for land armies, ferrying them around and keeping them supplied. To meet these needs, for many centuries Rome kept a moderate-size fleet of biremes and triremes, having two and three banks of oars, respectively, which were lighter and easier to maneuver than quinqueremes.

Although one important offensive tactic of such vessels was to ram and sink enemy ships, the Romans also sought to board and capture them, and they employed some special naval inventions designed to increase their chances of doing so. One was the *corvus*, or crow, consisting of a heavy wooden gangway that stood upright on a Roman deck until dropped onto an enemy deck. A metal spike at the end of the crow held the ships together while a force of Roman soldiers ran across the gangway. Though very effective in combat, a crow made a ship top-heavy, especially in rough weather, and the Romans lost tens of thousands of sailors when ships capsized during storms. This led Rome to abandon the device shortly before the end of the First Punic War. Two centuries later, Marcus Agrippa, Augustus Caesar's friend and war minister, attacked the problem with a fresh approach, inventing a special naval grappling hook with a long rope attached. When shot from a catapult, the hook caught an enemy ship and reeled it in for the kill.

Roman warships like this trireme, featuring three banks of oars, helped to defeat Carthage in the huge sea battles of the First Punic War.

the *aquila*, or silver eagle, the symbol for an entire legion. Next came the *optio*, equivalent of a modern-day sergeant, who was second in command to a centurion, who himself had charge of a century. Above the centurions stood the commander of the whole legion, the *legatus legionis* (usually appointed by the Senate, an emperor, or a general), and above them all the army's commanding general.

The Melting Pot and the Anvil

Thanks to this well-developed and efficient apparatus of training, discipline, weapons skills, strategy, and division of authority, the mighty Roman military conquered the Mediterranean world, made that world a Roman one, and ruled it for many centuries. When the Roman colossus finally fell, it was, to a significant degree, the result of the breakdown and failure of that military complex. In the fourth and fifth centuries A.D., increasing numbers of recruits came from distant provinces, especially from the northern German borderlands. These tribal peoples, whom the Italian Romans referred to as "barbarians," felt little allegiance to a faraway city called Rome, which most had never seen; so, as the army ranks swelled with their numbers, discipline and loyalty to the state inevitably and steadily declined.

In addition to the weakening of the military, Rome suffered from a long series of devastating social upheavals, as well as relentless and crippling political and economic decay. "A great civilization is not conquered from without until it has destroyed itself [from] within,"[138] Will Durant shrewdly observed. By the fifth century, Rome was a pale and pathetic shadow of the powerful and prosperous ruler of the *Pax Romana*. It was this weakened shell of an empire that had to face its greatest challenge—a massive onslaught of invasions by waves of new northern barbarians, among them the savage Huns, Vandals, and Goths. After numerous battles and massacres, devastation of whole regions, and a general breakdown of state authority, finances, and services, in A.D. 476 the last Roman emperor was forced from his throne and the Roman Empire simply ceased to exist as an entity.

But Rome left behind an important cultural heritage, and thereby many aspects of everyday Roman life and thought indirectly

The Goths sack Rome in the fifth century A.D. The Roman army, having become weak, disorganized, and poorly led, was powerless to stop them.

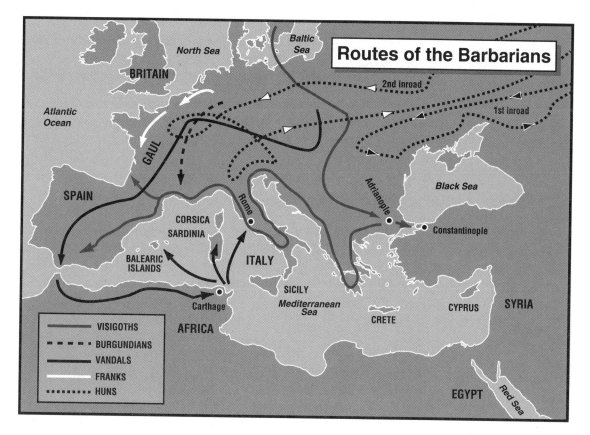

Routes of the Barbarians

survived to inspire later Western societies. "This is the essential accomplishment of Rome," wrote Durant.

Having won the Mediterranean world she adopted its culture, gave it order, prosperity, and peace for 200 years [the *Pax Romana*] . . . and transmitted the classic heritage to the West before she died. . . . She absorbed with appreciation and preserved with tenacity, the technical, intellectual, and artistic heritage that she had received from Carthage and Egypt, Greece and the East.[139]

In a very real sense, Rome was a melting pot of words, customs, styles, inventions, and ideas from many lands. The Romans bor-

rowed, translated, improved, and perfected these, and then, after reinterpreting them within the majestic framework of Roman law, applied them with fresh vigor to their own lives.

As the so-called barbarians who overran Rome absorbed many of these facets of a dead nation, they themselves were slowly yet relentlessly and beneficially transformed. On the anvil of Roman life and law they forged the European nations that subsequently carried the torch of civilization into the modern world. As Grant aptly puts it, the world of ancient Rome was "both wonderful and horrible, as startling and enlightened in many ways as it was gray and brutish in others. But it was a world which we can scarcely ignore, since in many ways it made us what we are."[140]

Notes

Introduction: Rome's Blueprint for Success

1. Quoted in Garry Wills, ed., *Roman Culture: Weapons and the Man*. New York: George Braziller, 1966, p. 245.
2. Quoted in Wills, *Roman Culture*, p. 243.
3. Polybius, *The Histories*, vol. 1. Translated by W. R. Paton. Cambridge, MA: Harvard University Press, 1966, p.55.
4. Edith Hamilton, *The Roman Way to Western Civilization*. New York: W. W. Norton, 1932, p. 116.
5. Harold Mattingly, *The Man in the Roman Street*. New York: W. W. Norton, 1966, p. 49.
6. Quoted in Stringfellow Barr, *The Mask of Jove: A History of Graeco-Roman Civilization from the Death of Alexander to the Death of Constantine*. Philadelphia: J. B. Lippincott, 1966, p. 61.
7. Michael Grant, *A Social History of Greece and Rome*. New York: Charles Scribner's Sons, 1992, p. 127.
8. Quoted in Michael Grant, *The World of Rome*. New York: New American Library, 1960, p. 57.

Chapter 1: Rungs on the Social Ladder: The People of the Roman State

9. R. H. Barrow, *The Romans*. Baltimore: Penguin Books, 1949, p. 45.
10. Grant, *A Social History of Greece and Rome*, pp. 49-50.
11. Grant, *A Social History of Greece and Rome*, p. 50.
12. Walton B. McDaniel, *Roman Private Life and Its Survivals*. New York: Cooper Square Publishers, 1963, p. 25.
13. Harold W. Johnston, *The Private Life of the Romans*. New York: Cooper Square Publishers, 1973, p. 31.
14. Public records dating from the reign of the emperor Trajan in the second century A.D. include lists of poor children needing public assistance. One town recorded 145 boys but only 34 girls. Since naturally occurring births would result in nearly equal numbers of boys and girls, exposure of several female babies is likely.
15. J. P. V. D. Balsdon, *Life and Leisure in Ancient Rome*. New York: McGraw-Hill, 1969, p. 86.
16. Quoted in Grant, *A Social History of Greece and Rome*, p. 27.
17. Pliny the Younger, *Letters*, vol. 2. Translated by William Melmouth. Cambridge, MA: Harvard University Press, 1961, p. 13.
18. Johnston, *The Private Life of the Romans*, pp. 72–73.
19. See Pliny the Elder, *Natural History*. Translated by H. Rackham. Cambridge, MA: Harvard University Press, 1967, XXXIII, p. 135.
20. Leonardo B. Dal Maso, *Rome of the Caesars*. Translated by Michael Hollingworth. Rome: Bonechi-Edizioni, n.d., p. 124.
21. Quoted in James Michie, ed. and trans., *The Epigrams of Martial*. New York: Random House, 1972, p. 89.
22. Paul Veyne, ed., *From Pagan Rome to Byzantium*, vol. 1 of Philippe Ariès and Georges Duby, eds., *A History of Private Life*. Cambridge, MA: Harvard University Press, 1987, p. 82.
23. Johnston, *The Private Life of the Romans*, p. 51.

24. Johnston, *The Private Life of the Romans*, p. 54.

Chapter 2: The Mind and Heart of the State: Roman Government and Law

25. Mattingly, *The Man in the Roman Street*, p. 141.
26. Chester G. Starr, *The Ancient Romans*. New York: Oxford University Press, 1971, p. 56.
27. The Romans took this principle very seriously. When the powerful general Julius Caesar declared himself dictator for life in February 44 B.C., he put himself on a collision course with the Senate, some members of which stabbed him to death a month later on the famous "Ides of March."
28. Starr, *The Ancient Romans*, p. 15.
29. Veyne, *From Pagan Rome to Byzantium*, p. 174.
30. Quoted in Grant, *The World of Rome*, pp. 104–105.
31. Quoted in Grant, *The World of Rome*, p. 105.
32. Mattingly, *The Man in the Roman Street*, p. 104.
33. Hamilton, *The Roman Way*, pp. 111–12.
34. Grant, *The World of Rome*, p. 101.
35. Quoted in Wills, *Roman Culture*, p. 285.
36. Quoted in Paul J. Alexander, ed., *The Ancient World: To 300 A.D.* New York: Macmillan, 1963, pp. 202–204.
37. In fact, because prosecuting or defending a person afforded an *advocatus* so much public exposure, the law profession became a way for well-to-do young men to enter the political arena. For example, the famous statesman and orator Cicero began as a lawyer in the courts, where he perfected his renowned gift for public speaking.
38. Quoted in William G. Sinnegin, ed., *Sources in Western Civilization: Rome*. New York: The Free Press, 1965, pp. 177–83.

Chapter 3: Two Worlds Intertwined: Country Life Versus City Life

39. Joan Liversidge, *Everyday Life in the Roman Empire*. New York: G. P. Putnam's Sons, 1976, p. 128.
40. For example, the ancient Jewish historian Flavius Josephus reported that in the first century A.D. the rural inhabitants of Roman Egypt numbered 7.5 million. This is more than twelve times the population of Alexandria at the time. Roman Italy was considerably more urbanized in the same period, yet out of a population of perhaps 7 to 8 million it is doubtful that more than 2 million lived in towns the size of Pompeii or larger.
41. Veyne, *From Pagan Rome to Byzantium*, p. 186.
42. Wills, *Roman Culture*, p. 24.
43. Virgil, *Eclogue I*, lines 46–56, in *Works*, vol. 1. Translated by H. Rushton Fairclough. Cambridge, MA: Harvard University Press, 1967, p. 7.
44. Johnston, *The Private Life of the Romans*, p. 203.
45. Veyne, *From Pagan Rome to Byzantium*, p. 117.
46. Liversidge, *Everyday Life*, p. 32.
47. Jerome Carcopino, *Daily Life in Ancient Rome: The People and the City at the Height of the Empire*. New Haven, CT: Yale University Press, 1940, pp. 48–49.
48. Quoted in G. G. Ramsay, trans., *Works of Juvenal and Persius*. Cambridge,

MA: Harvard University Press, 1965, p. 51.

49. In an attempt to reduce overcrowding in streets in the daytime, in the first century B.C. Julius Caesar initiated a law allowing most wheeled vehicles in the streets only at night. The law was renewed often in later centuries.

50. Juvenal, *Satires*, translated by Peter Green and excerpted in Bernard Knox, ed., *The Norton Book of Classical Literature*. New York: W. W. Norton, 1993, p. 824.

51. Some historians estimate even larger volumes of water. The respected Italian archaeologist Senatore R. Lanciani, for instance, suggests a total inflow of 475 million gallons a day.

52. Quoted in Donald R. Dudley, *The Romans: 850 B.C.–A.D. 337*. New York: Knopf, 1970, p. 147.

Chapter 4: Lifestyles of the Haves and Have-Nots: Homes and Their Contents

53. Quoted in Knox, *The Norton Book of Classical Literature*, p. 824.

54. Susan McKeever, *Ancient Rome*. London: Dorling Kindersley, 1995, p. 68.

55. Pliny the Younger, *Letters*, vol. 1, p. 153.

56. Pliny the Younger, *Letters*, vol. 1, pp. 163–65.

57. For those who could afford it, a few *insulae*, usually located in better neighborhoods, had larger *cenaculae*, some occupying half or even a full floor.

58. Quoted in Knox, *The Norton Book of Classical Literature*, p. 823.

59. Peter James and Nick Thorpe, *Ancient Inventions*. New York: Ballantine Books, 1994, p. 445. For a more comprehensive discussion of latrines and

sanitation, see Carcopino, *Daily Life in Ancient Rome*, pp. 40–42.

60. Quoted in Michie, *The Epigrams of Martial*, p. 169.

61. Quoted in Ramsay, *Works of Juvenal and Persius*, p. 53.

62. Quoted in Carcopino, *Daily Life in Ancient Rome*, p. 43.

63. The term *atrium* is derived from the Latin word *ater*, meaning "black," a reference to the fact that in Rome's earliest years the atrium was the main living room of a house. The walls of that room were invariably blackened by smoke from the hearth.

64. Johnston, *The Private Life of the Romans*, p. 135.

65. Colleen McCullough, *The First Man in Rome*. New York: William Morrow, 1990, p. 821.

66. Quoted in Michie, *The Epigrams of Martial*, p. 185.

67. Johnston, *The Private Life of the Romans*, pp. 169–70.

68. Liversidge, *Everyday Life*, p. 47.

69. Carcopino, *Daily Life in Ancient Rome*, p. 265.

70. Quoted in Ramsay, *Works of Juvenal and Persius*, pp. 75–77.

Chapter 5: "A Bald Head with Dressed Hair": Social Customs and Institutions

71. Quoted in F. R. Cowell, *Life in Ancient Rome*. New York: G. P. Putnam's Sons, 1961, p. 150.

72. Quoted in Michie, *The Epigrams of Martial*, p. 173.

73. Quoted in Ramsay, *Works of Juvenal and Persius*, p. 45.

74. Carcopino, *Daily Life in Ancient Rome*, pp. 157–58.

75. Quoted in Carcopino, *Daily Life in Ancient Rome*, p. 159.

76. Quoted in James and Thorpe, *Ancient Inventions*, p. 244.

77. Many Roman women also carried a "pocket set," or portable grooming kit, usually on a ring attached to their belts, when away from home. A typical example contained tweezers, a nail cleaner, an ear cleaner similar to a modern Q-tip, a toothpick to remove food particles from the teeth after a visit to a snack bar, as well as a small mirror and various makeup items.

78. Veyne, *From Pagan Rome to Byzantium*, p. 40.

79. Quoted in Wills, *Roman Culture*, p. 130.

80. Quoted in Carcopino, *Daily Life in Ancient Rome*, p. 100.

81. McCullough, *The First Man in Rome*, pp. 852–53.

82. Grant, *The World of Rome*, p. 92.

83. Quoted in Will Durant, *Caesar and Christ: A History of Roman Civilization and of Christianity from Their Beginnings to A.D. 325*. New York: Simon & Schuster, 1944, pp. 307–308.

84. Quoted in Durant, *Caesar and Christ*, p. 309.

85. James and Thorpe, *Ancient Inventions*, pp. 36–37.

Chapter 6: Bread and Circuses: Leisure Pursuits and Entertainments

86. Balsdon, *Life and Leisure in Ancient Rome*, pp. 268–69.

87. Johnston, *The Private Life of the Romans*, p. 291.

88. McKeever, *Ancient Rome*, p. 100.

89. Quoted in Michie, *The Epigrams of Martial*, p. 45.

90. Quoted in Michie, *The Epigrams of Martial*, p. 103.

91. Carcopino, *Daily Life in Ancient Rome*, p. 271.

92. Quoted in Ramsay, *Works of Juvenal and Persius*, p. 119. The phrase *vomunt ut edant, edunt ut vomant*, roughly translated as "vomit in order to eat, eat in order to vomit," was a common Roman adage.

93. Lionel Casson, *Masters of Ancient Comedy*. New York: Macmillan, 1960, p. 181.

94. Liversidge, *Everyday Life*, p. 95.

95. Quoted in Balsdon, *Life and Leisure in Ancient Rome*, p. 275.

96. By the third or fourth century A.D., as many as two hundred thousand people regularly received grain and other foodstuffs via some 2,300 distribution centers, all under the direction of the *Praefectus Annonae*, or minister of supply.

97. Carcopino, *Daily Life in Ancient Rome*, pp. 202–203 and 210.

98. Quoted in Kevin Guinagh and Alfred Paul Dorjahn, eds., *Latin Literature in Translation*. New York: Longman's, Green, 1952, p. 738.

99. The original name of the building was the *Amphitheatrum Flavium*, or Amphitheater of the Flavians, referring to the fact that the emperors Vespasian, who began it, and his son Titus, who completed it, were members of the Flavian family line. The name "Colosseum" was coined by medieval Europeans some five hundred years after Rome's fall.

100. The most spectacular example of a *velarium* was the purple one that covered the Theater of Pompey in A.D. 66. It featured a giant painting of the emperor Nero driving a chariot through the heavens.

101. Quoted in Grant, *The World of Rome*, p. 144.

102. Carcopino, *Daily Life in Ancient Rome*, p. 243.

103. Rowell, *Rome in the Augustan Age*, pp. 160–61.

Chapter 7: Supermarket of the World: Shipping, Trade, and Commerce

104. M. I. Finley, *The Ancient Economy*. Berkeley: University of California Press, 1985, p. 30.

105. Quoted in J. D. Kaplan, ed., *The Dialogues of Plato*. Translated by Benjamin Jowett. New York: Pocket Books, 1950, p. 148.

106. In the early Empire, Rome annually imported up to half a million tons of wheat. Most of it arrived at Ostia, on the south side of the Tiber's mouth, or at Portus, the port built by the emperor Claudius in the A.D. 40s on the north side. Workers transferred the grain to barges, which oxen towed upstream to Rome.

107. Quoted in Sinnegin, *Sources in Western Civilization*, p. 175.

108. Lionel Casson, *The Ancient Mariners*. New York: Macmillan, 1959, p. 226.

109. Quoted in Grant, *The World of Rome*, p. 80.

110. Quoted in Basil Davenport, ed. and trans., *The Portable Roman Reader: The Culture of the Roman State*. New York: Viking Press, 1951, pp. 560–61.

111. Quoted in Casson, *The Ancient Mariners*, pp. 235–36.

112. Veyne, *From Pagan Rome to Byzantium*, pp. 189–90.

113. Roman coins were also minted to commemorate special events. A famous example is the silver coin minted in 42 B.C. by the senators who assassinated Julius Caesar two years before. The coin bore the image of Brutus, one of the senators, on one side. On the other side were two daggers, representing the murder weapons, and the words *EID MAR*, which stood for the Ides of March, or March 15, the date of the murder.

114. Durant, *Caesar and Christ*, p. 331.

Chapter 8: Diverse Paths to Heavenly Truths: Roman Religious Beliefs

115. Quoted in Starr, *The Ancient Romans*, p. 19.

116. Arthur E. R. Boak, *A History of Rome to 565 A.D.* New York: Macmillan, 1943, pp. 96–97.

117. Mattingly, *The Man in the Roman Street*, p. 73.

118. Mattingly, *The Man in the Roman Street*, p. 73.

119. The concept of "three" as having a special significance in a triad or trinity of gods or spirits is common to many religions, past and present. Other examples include the Christian Trinity comprised of Father, Son, and Holy Ghost, and the Hindu *Trimurti*, or Three Shapes, manifested by the gods Brahma, the Creator; Vishnu, the Preserver; and Shiva, the Destroyer.

120. Quoted in Ramsay, *Works of Juvenal and Persius*, p. 191.

121. Liversidge, *Everyday Life*, p. 183.

122. Quoted in Ramsay, *Works of Juvenal and Persius*, p. 335.

123. Quoted in Meyer Reinhold, *Essentials of Greek and Roman Classics*. Great Neck, NY: Barron's Educational Series, 1946, pp. 318–19.

124. Mattingly, *The Man in the Roman Street*, p. 56.

125. Quoted in Wills, *Roman Culture*, p. 364.
126. Quoted in Durant, *Caesar and Christ*, p. 389.
127. Quoted in Ramsay, *Works of Juvenal and Persius*, p. 253.
128. Apuleius, quoted in Grant, *The World of Rome*, p. 198.

Chapter 9: Marching the Paths of Glory: Life in the Roman Army

129. Michael Grant, *The Army of the Caesars*. New York: M. Evans, 1974, p. xv.
130. Quoted in Casson, *The Ancient Mariners*, p. 212.
131. Quoted in Reinhold, *Essentials of Greek and Roman Classics*, p. 319.
132. Quoted in Ramsay, *Works of Juvenal and Persius*, pp. 303–305.
133. Lionel Casson, *Daily Life in Ancient Rome*. New York: American Heritage, 1975, p. 72.
134. One reason that Augustus established these generous pensions was to discourage attempts by popular generals to award such bonuses on their own in order to win over the allegiance of their soldiers and thereby to create their own private armies. Under Marius, Caesar, and other power-hungry generals who had challenged the state, this practice had helped to bring down the Republic.
135. Casson, *Daily Life*, p. 73.
136. Grant, *The Army of the Caesars*, p. xviii.
137. Flavius Josephus, *Works*. Translated by William Whiston. Edinburgh: William P. Nimmo, n.d., p. 505.
138. Durant, *Caesar and Christ*, p. 665.
139. Durant, *Caesar and Christ*, pp. 670–71.
140. Grant, *The World of Rome*, p. 320.

Glossary

advocatus: A lawyer.

aediles: Government officials who supervised public buildings, markets, and roads, and also organized public games and entertainments.

ager publicus: "Public lands"; territories taken by Rome during its many conquests and later leased or sold by the state to Roman citizens.

aliptae: Attendants, often slaves or freedmen, who gave massages in private baths, wrestling schools, or private residences.

animism: A belief system in which inanimate objects and forces are thought to be inhabited by thinking spirits.

apodyterium: In a bathhouse, a room for undressing and dressing.

apophoreta: Leftovers from a meal.

aqua: Water; when capitalized, a particular aqueduct, for instance, the Aqua Virgo.

aquila: "Eagle"; Rome's chief identifying symbol; also, a silver eagle used as the symbol for an army legion.

aquilifer: A soldier who bore his legion's *aquila* and other standards.

aratrum: A wooden plow, sometimes equipped with an iron blade.

argentarius (plural, argentarii): A banker.

as (plural, asses): A copper coin worth one-fourth of a *sestertius*.

astrology: A system of belief that advocates that the heavenly bodies exert a direct influence on people's lives.

atrium: The front foyer and meeting place of a well-to-do house.

auctoritas: Moral authority.

aureus: The most valuable Roman coin, composed of about a quarter ounce of gold.

auxilia: Military forces, consisting of noncitizens recruited from the provinces, that supplemented the regular Roman legions.

a veste forensi: Slaves in charge of the emperor's city clothes; *a veste gladiatoria*, of his theater clothes; *a veste privata*, of his palace clothes; *a veste triumphali*, of his parade uniforms.

balneatores: Bath attendants, often slaves or freedmen.

basilica: A large building, with an open central plaza, used for court trials and public meetings.

bireme: A ship having two banks of oars.

caldarium: In a bathhouse, a "hot" room containing one or more warm pools.

Campus Martius: The Field of Mars; in ancient Rome, a large open area lined with imposing public buildings and used for large public gatherings and ceremonies.

candelabrae: Tall, decorative stands that held oil lamps or candles.

Capitol: Common name for Rome's Capitoline hill, on which rested the famous Temple of Jupiter.

Capitolium: The Temple of Jupiter, dedicated to the gods Jupiter, Juno, and Minerva, members of the Capitoline Triad, and located atop the Capitoline hill.

cella: A temple's main room, in which rested the cult image, or statue, of the god to whom the building was dedicated.

cena: Supper; the main meal.

cenacula (plural, cenaculae): An apartment within an *insula*.

censores: Censors; public officials charged with supervising the membership of the Senate and also with awarding state contracts for buildings and roads.

Centuriate Assembly: The legislative body originally composed of aristocrats, wealthy persons, and members of ancient and prominent families.

centuries: Individual wards or precincts making up the Roman assemblies; also, groups of soldiers, at first containing one hundred men each and later containing eighty.

citrarii: Cabinetmakers.

cives: Citizens.

clientes: Clients.

cognomen (plural, cognomina): A Roman's family name.

cognomen ex virtute: A special honorary title awarded to outstanding statesmen and military generals.

cohort: A tactical fighting unit, usually consisting of about five hundred men, used in Roman armies of the late Republic and thereafter.

cohortes urbanae: "Urban battalions"; Rome's police force, instituted by the emperor Augustus.

collegia: Colleges; private associations or clubs whose members, exclusively men, practiced a common trade.

coloni (singular, colonus): Tenant farmers who worked on large estates owned by others.

colonnade: A row of columns; or a column-lined roofed walkway.

columbarii: Underground vaults that held urns filled with human ashes.

compluvium: The opening in an atrium's roof.

consul: In the Republic, one of two jointly serving chief government administrators who also commanded the armies; their office was the consulship, and matters pertaining to it or them were termed consular.

contubernium (plural, contubernia): An army unit composed of eight men who shared the same tent and traveled and ate together.

corvus: "Crow," or "raven"; a naval warfare device, consisting of a wooden gangway with a spike protruding from the end, which stood upright on a Roman deck until dropped onto an enemy deck, at which time the spike penetrated the deck and held the ships together while Roman soldiers ran across and boarded the other vessel.

crepida: A sandal.

curator aquarum: Rome's water commissioner, in charge of aqueducts and sewers.

denarius (plural, denarii): A silver coin worth one twenty-fifth of an *aureus*.

desultores: Stunt charioteers who performed acrobatics.

dignitas: Prestige.

domus: A private house or houses, usually of the well-to-do.

do ut des: A phrase expressing the relationship between an individual and the gods, roughly translated as "I, the mortal, give to you, the god, so that you may give back to me."

Elysium: Heaven; the section of the underworld reserved for the souls of virtuous people.

equestrians: Well-to-do businessmen who constituted a non-land-based aristocracy second in prestige only to the landowning patricians.

exposure: The practice of abandoning an infant outside to die.

fabri lignarii: Woodworkers.

fabula saltica: The art or performance of Roman pantomime, which was similar to modern ballet.

falx: A sickle used to harvest wheat.

familia: The family.

feriae: Religious festivals; or the holidays on which they were celebrated.

fibulae: Decorative fastening pins.

foricae: Public latrines.

forum: A city's main square, used for public gatherings and as a marketplace.

Forum Romanum: Rome's original forum.

frigidarium: In a bathhouse, a "cold" room containing one or more cold pools.

genius: The special guardian spirit thought to inhabit the body of a family's paterfamilias and to pass on, when he died, to his son, thus ensuring the continuity of the family line.

gens **(plural,** *gentes***):** An ancient tribal clan.

Hades: The underworld.

harpastum: A rough-and-tumble ball game similar to rugby.

herm: A bust of the Greek god Hermes (the Roman god Mercury) set outside the front door of a house to discourage evil from entering.

hypocaust: A heating system in which hot air from a furnace circulated through brick conduits into an open space beneath a building.

imago: A lifelike mask representing a family's most prestigious ancestor.

imperium: Supreme power.

impluvium: The basin resting in an atrium beneath the *compluvium.*

insula **(plural,** *insulae***):** A city block; or, a multistoried apartment building occupying such a block.

judex: A judge.

judices: Jurors.

judicium: A court trial.

Juno: The goddess who protected women; also, the special guardian spirit thought to inhabit the body of a family's materfamilias and to pass on, when she died, to her daughter.

laconicum: In a bathhouse, a sauna, or warm and dry room.

lararium: In a *domus*, a small shrine or altar for praying to the family spirits.

lares: Spirits thought to keep a home safe and also to guard streets and crossroads.

lasani **(singular,** *lasanum***):** Chamber pots or bedpans.

latifundia **(singular,** *latifundium***):** Large farming estates usually owned by absentee landlords and worked by slaves and tenant farmers.

Latins: The tribal people from whom the Romans were descended.

Latium: The fertile plain, situated between the Tiber River and the Apennines, that constituted the original Roman homeland.

lectus: A couch, sofa, or recliner.

legatus legionis: A military officer in command of a legion.

legion: An army battalion, consisting at first of about 4,200 men and later of 5,000 to 6,000 men.

lex Aquilia: A law holding doctors responsible for negligence; ***lex Cornelia:*** A law providing punishment for doctors whose carelessness caused the death of a patient.

libertus: A freedman, or slave who has gained his freedom.

lucerna **(plural,** ***lucernae***)**:** An oil lamp.

ludi: Large-scale public shows; or the holidays these shows celebrated; ***ludi circenses:*** Chariot races.

ludus: Elementary school; ***ludus saltatorius:*** Dancing classes.

luxus: Luxury.

magister **(plural,** ***magistri***)**:** Schoolteacher; also used to describe chief officials, managers, and superintendents of various kinds, including the local officials who managed Rome's *vici*, or wards.

manes: Household spirits of deceased ancestors, thought to watch over various family members.

maniple: A tactical fighting unit, usually consisting of about 120 men, used in Rome's early republican armies.

mansiones: Guest houses located along Roman roads.

mare nostrum: "Our sea"; the name the Romans gave to the Mediterranean after gaining control of all of its lands and peoples.

marita: A wife.

maritus: A husband.

materfamilias (plural, matresfamilias): The wife or mother of the paterfamilias.

matrimonium **(plural,** ***matrimonii***)**:** Marriage.

mensa publica: Money-changing tables set up in marketplaces and other public areas.

meretrix: A female prostitute.

meta: A millstone.

micatio: A gambling game in which a player tried to guess how many fingers his or her opponent raised.

mime: A short comedic theatrical skit, often obscene; or an actor who performed such skits.

"Morituri te salutamus!": "We who are about to die salute you!"; the phrase recited by gladiators just prior to combat.

munera: Private or public shows featuring gladiatorial and/or animal combats.

murmillo: A gladiator equipped with a helmet, shield, and sword.

naumachia: Full-scale mock sea battles staged in flooded amphitheaters or artificial lakes.

nomen (plural, nomina): A Roman's clan name.

numina: Spirits, or minor deities, including the *lares*, *penates*, and *manes*, who watched over various aspects of human life.

oligarchy: A government controlled by a small group of individuals.

optimus princeps: The "best citizen," or "best of princes"; a title often accorded to Roman emperors.

optio: An army sergeant, second in command to a centurion.

ornatores: Hairdressers, often slaves or freedmen.

paedagogus: A slave or freedman employed by a family to accompany the children to school.

palaestrae: Gyms or wrestling areas, often housed in public bathhouses.

Palatine: One of Rome's seven hills, on which rested the lavish residences of the emperors.

palla: An outer cloak worn by women.

"panem et circenses": "Bread and circuses"; the term referring to the state's sponsorship of free food and public shows to appease the idle masses.

pantomimus (plural, *pantomimae*): An actor who performed in a pantomime.

paterfamilias (plural, patresfamilias): The male head of a Roman family.

patres: Fathers; the Roman state's leading men, usually wealthy landowners heading the most powerful and respected families.

patria potestas: The traditional power and authority held by the paterfamilias over the members of his household.

patricians: Members of Rome's wealthiest and most privileged class.

patronage: The system in which one individual, the client, gave homage to and did favors for a wealthier and more powerful person, the patron, in exchange for financial and legal protection.

patroni: Patrons.

Pax Romana: "Great Roman Peace"; the highly peaceful and prosperous era roughly encompassed by the first and second centuries A.D.

penates: Spirits thought to protect a family's food storage.

peregrini: Foreigners.

peristylum: In a *domus*, a walled garden, usually lined with colonnades.

pilum: A javelin, or throwing spear.

pistor (plural, *pistores*): A combination miller and baker.

pluvia: Rain.

podex: A mild obscenity referring to the rear end.

pompa: A procession or parade.

pons: A bridge or bridges.

pontifex maximus: The office of the chief priest of the Roman religion; or, the person holding that office.

pontiffs: Head priests or religious officials.

praenomen (plural, praenomina): A Roman's first name, identifying him or her as an individual.

praetors: In the Republic, government officials who managed the legal system and also administered the city when the consuls were away.

prandium: Lunch.

provincials: Residents of the Roman provinces.

puer: Boy; the corrupted slang version, *por*, was used to identify slaves.

pulpitum: The stage in a Roman theater.

pulvinar: In an arena, the imperial box, or special seating area reserved for the emperor and other notables.

quadrans: A copper coin equal to one-fourth of an *as*, or one-sixteenth of a *sestertius*.

quadrigarum (plural, *quadrigae*): A chariot drawn by four horses.

quaestors: Public officials in charge of financial matters.

quinquereme: A warship having either five banks of oars or five rowers to an oar.

regiones: The fourteen districts into which Augustus Caesar organized the city of Rome.

retiarius: A gladiator who fought with a net and a long trident.

rhetoric: The art of persuasive speech and public oratory.

River Styx: The river thought to mark the boundary between the world of the living and the underworld.

saltatrix tonsa: A male prostitute who dressed as a woman.

sarcophagi (singular, sarcophagus): Coffins.

scaenae frons: In a Roman theater, the wall behind the stage on which scenery was painted or hung.

schola (or grammaticus): Secondary school.

scutum: A soldier's rectangular shield.

Senate: The Roman legislative body, made up of well-to-do aristocrats, that, during the Republic, directed foreign policy, advised the consuls, and in general controlled the state.

senatores: The community fathers who formed the advisory council to the original Roman kings, a body that later became the Senate.

sestertius (plural, sestertii or sesterces): A silver or bronze coin equal originally to 2.5 and later to 4 *asses*; also equal to one-fourth of a *denarius*.

sicarii: Murderers.

signifer: A soldier who bore his century's standards.

speculares: Transparent glass panes.

spina: The long stone axis, decorated with obelisks and statues, that ran down the center of a Roman circus.

SPQR: Rome's official symbol, which stood for *Senatus Populusque Romanus*, "The Senate and People of Rome."

stibium: A black mixture of powdered antimony and water used as an eyeliner.

stola: An ankle-length dress or tunic worn by women.

taberna (plural, tabernae): A small shop or merchant's booth; or an inn or tavern; or a poor cottage.

tablinum: A study, usually used by the master of a *domus*.

talis: Dice, or a game played with dice.

Tartarus: A section of the underworld where sinners suffered eternal punishment.

tepidarium: In a bathhouse, a warm room in which a person waited briefly before bathing in order to reduce the discomfort of passing too suddenly from the colder air outside the bathhouse into the muggy air in the heated rooms within.

testudo: "Turtle," or "tortoise"; a squared, tightly packed military formation in which soldiers held their shields overhead, creating a barrier to enemy missiles.

thermarum (plural, thermae): A public bathhouse.

thermopolium (plural, thermopolii): Fast-food shops or snack bars.

Thracian: A native of the region of Thrace in Greece; or a Roman gladiator who fought with a small round shield and short curved sword, traditional weapons of the early Thracians.

toga: The standard Roman formal outfit, consisting of a large oblong piece of cloth wrapped and folded around the body in various ways; the *toga alba* was white and plain, the *toga praetexta* had a purple border, the *toga picta* was all purple with gold trim, and the *toga pulla* was black.

tonsor (plural, tonsores): Barber, either independent or privately employed.

tonstrina: A barbershop.

Tribal Assembly: The legislative body composed of common plebs, which passed measures called plebiscites.

tribune: A public official elected by the Tribal Assembly who could nullify any unjust law proposed by either assembly by declaring "Veto," or "I forbid"; tribunes could also arrest any citizen suspected of wrongdoing, including consuls.

tribunician powers: The powers held by the tribunes.

triclinium: A dining room.

trireme: A ship having three banks of oars.

Twelve Tables (or Tablets): Rome's original set of laws, first written down in the fifth century B.C.

unctorium: In a bathhouse, a room in which people rubbed themselves with oil after bathing.

velarium: An awning, such as the kind stretched over the top of a theater or amphitheater.

via (plural, viae): A public road, usually paved.

vici (singular, vicus): Subdivisions of Rome's *regiones*, similar to modern wards and precincts.

villa: A comfortable country house or manor.

vomitoria: The entranceways/exitways in theaters and stadiums.

For Further Reading

Isaac Asimov, *The Roman Empire*. Boston: Houghton Mifflin, 1967. An excellent, easy-to-read, although brief and general, overview of all aspects of imperial Roman history.

Lionel Casson, *Daily Life in Ancient Rome*. New York: American Heritage, 1975. A fascinating presentation of how the Romans lived: their homes, streets, entertainments, eating habits, marriage customs, and so on.

Ron Goor and Nancy Goor, *Pompeii: Exploring a Roman Ghost Town*. New York: Thomas Y. Crowell, 1986. An overview of the excavations at Pompeii, a small Roman city that flourished in the first century A.D. and was buried by a volcanic eruption. For basic readers.

Rhoda A. Hendricks, trans., *Classical Gods and Heroes*. New York: Morrow Quill, 1974. A collection of easy-to-read translations of famous Greek and Roman myths and tales, as told by ancient Greek and Roman writers such as Homer in his *Iliad* and Ovid in his *Metamorphoses*.

Anthony Marks and Graham Tingay, *The Romans*. London: Usborne Publishing, 1990. Aimed at young readers, this is a very accurate and entertaining summary of Roman history and life, with hundreds of fine color illustrations.

Susan McKeever, *Ancient Rome*. London: Dorling Kindersley, 1995. This sketchy but handsomely mounted general introduction to ancient Roman culture contains much useful and fascinating information on topics such as clothing, shopping, country life, health and medicine, public buildings and waterworks, games, religious rites, and much more. Beautifully illustrated with color drawings.

Don Nardo, *The Roman Republic* and *The Roman Empire*. Both: San Diego: Lucent Books, 1994; *Greek and Roman Theater* and *The Punic Wars*. Both: San Diego: Lucent Books, 1995; *The Age of Augustus* and *The Importance of Julius Caesar*. Both: San Diego: Lucent Books, 1997; *The Battle of Actium*. San Diego: Lucent Books, forthcoming. These comprehensive but easy-to-read volumes provide a general overview of the important events and major political and military figures of Roman history. They can be seen as companion studies to this volume on everyday Roman life.

Major Works Consulted

J. P. V. D. Balsdon, *Life and Leisure in Ancient Rome*. New York: McGraw-Hill, 1969. In comprehensiveness, detail, and overall scholarship, this study of Roman life by a noted scholar is on a par with Jerome Carcopino's masterwork in the field.

Jerome Carcopino, *Daily Life in Ancient Rome: The People and the City at the Height of the Empire*. New Haven, CT: Yale University Press, 1940. An extremely well researched and entertaining scholarly study of Roman imperial customs, people, dress, food, games, religion, and much more. A classic of its kind.

Lionel Casson, *The Ancient Mariners*. New York: Macmillan, 1959. This magnificently researched and well-written study of trade, shipping, warfare, and other aspects of ancient ships, ports, and seamen is a modern classic and highly recommended for all.

F. R. Cowell, *Cicero and the Roman Republic*. Baltimore: Penguin Books, 1967. A very detailed and interesting analysis of the late Republic, its leaders, and the problems that eventually led to its collapse. This is one of the best available studies of the complexities and intrigues of Roman government and politics.

———, *Life in Ancient Rome*. New York: G. P. Putnam's Sons, 1961. One of the most noted modern experts on ancient Rome here offers a commendable, easy-to-read study of most aspects of Roman daily life. Highly recommended.

Basil Davenport, ed. and trans., *The Portable Roman Reader: The Culture of the Roman State*. New York: Viking Press, 1951. A thoughtful collection of Roman writings from all periods, with especially large sections devoted to the poems of Catullus, Horace, and Martial.

L. Sprague de Camp, *The Ancient Engineers*. New York: Ballantine Books, 1963. This famous and often reprinted book covers not only large engineering feats such as bridges, temples, and aqueducts, but also offers many revealing details about everyday Roman life, including the use of glass for windows, how nails were made and used, the dangers of lead water pipes, and much more.

Donald R. Dudley, *The Romans: 850 B.C.– A.D. 337*. New York: Knopf, 1970. A very thoughtful overview of Roman history and culture.

Jane F. Gardner, *Women in Roman Law and Society*. Indianapolis: Indiana University Press, 1986. An excellent study of women in Roman times. Highly recommended for those wishing to delve into some of the finer details of Roman life.

Michael Grant, *The Army of the Caesars*. New York: M. Evans, 1974. Grant's detailed study of the evolution of Roman armies, including military reforms by Caesar, Augustus, and other notables, is first-rate scholarship.

———, *A Social History of Greece and Rome*. New York: Charles Scribner's Sons, 1992. Another fine book by Grant, this study explores the ins and outs of ancient Roman social life and customs, including the role of women, rich versus poor, and the status of slaves and foreigners.

———, *The World of Rome*. New York: New American Library, 1960. A scholarly yet colorful and fascinating glimpse of Roman culture, with plenty of primary source quotations revealing much about Roman life. Considered by many a modern classic.

Peter James and Nick Thorpe, *Ancient Inventions*. New York: Ballantine Books, 1994. A fascinating study of the who, when, and how of thousands of everyday utensils, tools, weapons, personal belongings, foods, public institutions, habits, and ideas introduced by the ancients, including the Romans.

Harold W. Johnston, *The Private Life of the Romans*. New York: Cooper Square Publishers, 1973. An excellent, very detailed study of everyday Roman life, with an informative and useful abundance of Latin names, terms, and phrases, a feature often absent in similar works.

Joan Liversidge, *Everyday Life in the Roman Empire*. New York: G. P. Putnam's Sons, 1976. A well-researched and clearly written synopsis of most major aspects of Roman life, consistently supported by references to various archaeological discoveries.

James Michie, ed. and trans., *The Epigrams of Martial*. New York: Random House, 1972. This is a fine collection of some of the best of the often funny, sometimes blatantly obscene, and always wonderfully witty short poems of Marcus Valerius Martialis, known to posterity as Martial. These timeless gems reveal much about everyday Roman customs, attitudes, and love rituals.

G. G. Ramsay, trans., *Works of Juvenal and Persius*. Cambridge, MA: Harvard University Press, 1965. The satires of Decimus Junius Juvenalis, known as Juvenal, and Aulus Persius Flaccus, called Persius for short, capture many of the customs and attitudes, both admirable and despicable, of early imperial Rome. This is sometimes difficult reading for the uninitiated but a must for true fans of ancient Rome.

Henry Thompson Rowell, *Rome in the Augustan Age*. Norman: University of Oklahoma Press, 1962. A well-written synopsis of the history and culture of one of Rome's greatest periods, with a heavy emphasis on religious, social, and moral values.

William G. Sinnegin, ed., *Sources in Western Civilization: Rome*. New York: The Free Press, 1965. A fine collection of Roman writings, including excerpts from works by Livy, Polybius, Appian, Cicero, Suetonius, and others. Also contains the *Res Gestae*, the short but important work written by Augustus Caesar, the first and greatest Roman emperor.

Chester G. Starr, *The Ancient Romans*. New York: Oxford University Press, 1971. A well-written short summary of both the Roman Republic and the Roman Empire. Includes several interesting sidebars on topics such as religion, law, architecture, the Etruscans, and the Augustan Age.

Suetonius, *Lives of the Twelve Caesars*, published as *The Twelve Caesars*. Translated by Robert Graves and revised by Michael Grant. New York: Penguin Books, 1979. Suetonius's biographies of several of the Roman emperors reveal much about ancient Roman life, customs, and attitudes.

Garry Wills, ed., *Roman Culture: Weapons and the Man*. New York: George Braziller, 1966. This excellent collection of Latin literature contains works by Virgil, Horace, Ovid, Plautus, Propertius, Martial, Catullus, Cicero, Juvenal, Lucan, Tacitus, and many other important Roman writers. Also, Wills's long introduction contains much insightful commentary.

Additional Works Consulted

Frank F. Abbot, *Society and Politics in Ancient Rome: Essays and Sketches*. New York: Biblo and Tannen, 1963.

Paul J. Alexander, ed., *The Ancient World: To 300 A.D.* New York: Macmillan, 1963.

Appian, *Roman History*. 4 vols. Translated by Horace White. Cambridge, MA: Harvard University Press, 1964.

Apuleius, *The Golden Ass*. Translated by Robert Graves. New York: Farrar, Straus, and Young, 1951.

E. Badian, *Roman Imperialism in the Late Republic*. Ithaca, NY: Cornell University Press, 1968.

Stringfellow Barr, *The Mask of Jove: A History of Graeco-Roman Civilization from the Death of Alexander to the Death of Constantine*. Philadelphia: J. B. Lippincott, 1966.

R. H. Barrow, *The Romans*. Baltimore: Penguin Books, 1949.

Anthony Birley, trans., *Lives of the Later Caesars*. New York: Penguin Books, 1976.

Arthur E. R. Boak, *A History of Rome to 565 A.D.* New York: Macmillan, 1943.

Keith R. Bradley, *Discovering the Roman Family: Studies in Roman Social History*. New York: Oxford University Press, 1991.

James Henry Breasted, *Ancient Times: A History of the Early World*. Boston: Ginn, 1944.

James H. Butler, *The Theater and Drama of Greece and Rome*. San Francisco: Chandler Publishing, 1972.

Lionel Casson, *Masters of Ancient Comedy*. New York: Macmillan, 1960.

Gilbert Charles-Picard, *Augustus and Nero*. Translated (from the French) by Len Ortzen. New York: Thomas Y. Crowell, 1965.

Cicero, *Letters to Atticus*. 3 vols. Translated by E. O. Winstedt. Cambridge, MA: Harvard University Press, 1961.

Tim Cornell and John Matthews, *Atlas of the Roman World*. New York: Facts On File, 1982.

Leonardo B. Dal Maso, *Rome of the Caesars*. Translated by Michael Hollingworth. Rome: Bonechi-Edizioni, n.d.

Dio Cassius, *Roman History*. Translated by Ian Scott-Kilvert. New York: Penguin Books, 1987.

Robert B. Downs, *Books That Changed the World*. New York: Penguin Books, 1983.

George E. Duckworth, ed., *Roman Comedies*. New York: Random House, 1942.

Donald R. Dudley, *The Civilization of Rome*. New York: New American Library, 1960.

J. Wight Duff, *A Literary History of Rome from the Origins to the Close of the Golden Age*. New York: Barnes and Noble, 1963.

Will Durant, *Caesar and Christ: A History of Roman Civilization and of Christianity from Their Beginnings to A.D. 325*. New York: Simon & Schuster, 1944.

M. I. Finley, *The Ancient Economy*. Berkeley: University of California Press, 1985.

——, *Ancient Slavery and Modern Ideology*. New York: Penguin Books, 1980.

Frontius, *The Stratagems and the Aqueducts of Rome*. Translated by C. E. Bennett. Cambridge, MA: Harvard University Press, 1925.

Fronto, *Correspondence*. 2 vols. Translated by C. R. Haines. Cambridge, MA: Harvard University Press, 1919.

Marion Geisinger, *Plays, Players, and Playwrights: An Illustrated History of the Theater*. New York: Hart Publishing, 1971.

Michael Grant, *The Ancient Mediterranean*. New York: Penguin Books, 1969.

———, *History of Rome*. New York: Scribner's, 1978.

———, *The Myths of the Greeks and Romans*. New York: Penguin Books, 1962.

Kevin Guinagh and Alfred Paul Dorjahn, eds., *Latin Literature in Translation*. New York: Longman's, Green, 1952.

Edith Hamilton, *The Roman Way to Western Civilization*. New York: W. W. Norton, 1932.

W. G. Hardy, *The Greek and Roman World*. Cambridge, MA: Schenkman Publishing, 1960.

Ian Jenkins, *Greek and Roman Life*. Cambridge, MA: Harvard University Press, 1986.

Flavius Josephus, *Works*. Translated by William Whiston. Edinburgh: William P. Nimmo, n.d.

J. D. Kaplan, ed., *The Dialogues of Plato*. Translated by Benjamin Jowett. New York: Pocket Books, 1950.

Dorling Kindersley, ed., *Quest for the Past: Amazing Answers to the Riddles of History*. Pleasantville, NY: Reader's Digest Association, 1984.

Bernard Knox, ed., *The Norton Book of Classical Literature*. New York: W. W. Norton, 1993.

Senatore R. Lanciani, *Ancient and Modern Rome*. New York: Cooper Square Publishers, 1963.

Livy, *From the Founding of the City*. 14 vols. Translated by B. O. Foster. Cambridge, MA: Harvard University Press, 1967.

Harold Mattingly, *The Man in the Roman Street*. New York: W. W. Norton, 1966.

Colleen McCullough, *The First Man in Rome*. New York: William Morrow, 1990.

Walton B. McDaniel, *Roman Private Life and Its Survivals*. New York: Cooper Square Publishers, 1963.

Susan McKeever, *Ancient Rome*. London: Dorling Kindersley, 1995.

Pliny the Elder, *Natural History*. 10 vols. Translated by H. Rackham. Cambridge, MA: Harvard University Press, 1967.

Pliny the Younger, *Letters*. 2 vols. Translated by William Melmouth. Cambridge, MA: Harvard University Press, 1961.

Plutarch, *Lives of the Noble Grecians and Romans*. Translated by John Dryden. New York: Random House, 1932.

Plutarch, *Lives of the Noble Grecians and Romans*, excerpted in *Plutarch: Fall of the Roman Republic*. Translated by Rex Warner. Baltimore: Penguin Books, 1958.

Polybius, *The Histories*. Vol. 1. Translated by W. R. Paton. Cambridge, MA: Harvard University Press, 1966.

Quintilian, *The Education of an Orator*. Translated by H. E. Butler. Cambridge, MA: Harvard University Press, 1963.

Betty Radice, ed., *Pliny: Letters and Panegyricus*. Cambridge, MA: Harvard University Press, 1965.

————, *Who's Who in the Ancient World*. New York: Penguin Books, 1973.

Meyer Reinhold, *Essentials of Greek and Roman Classics*. Great Neck, NY: Barron's Educational Series, 1946.

Michael Simkins, *Warriors of Rome: An Illustrated History of the Roman Legions*. London: Blandford, 1988.

D. P. Simpson, *Cassell's Latin Dictionary*. New York: Macmillan, 1968.

Jon Solomon, *The Ancient World in the Cinema*. New York: A. S. Barnes, 1978.

Tacitus, *The Annals*, published as *The Annals of Imperial Rome*. Translated by Michael Grant. New York: Penguin Books, 1989.

Lily Ross Taylor, *Party Politics in the Age of Caesar*. Berkeley: University of California Press, 1968.

Charles Van Doren, *A History of Knowledge, Past, Present, and Future*. New York: Ballantine Books, 1991.

Paul Veyne, ed., *From Pagan Rome to Byzantium*, vol. 1 of Philippe Ariès and Georges Duby, eds., *A History of Private Life*. Cambridge, MA: Harvard University Press, 1987.

Michael Vickers, *The Roman World*. New York: Peter Bedrick Books, 1989.

Virgil, *Aeneid*. Translated by Patric Dickinson. New York: New American Library, 1961.

————, *Works*. 2 vols. Translated by H. Rushton Fairclough. Cambridge, MA: Harvard University Press, 1967.

Index

Picture Credits

Cover photo: AKG, London

Archibald Cary Coolidge Fund, Courtesy Museum of Fine Arts, Boston, 22

Archivi Alinari/Art Resource, NY, 71

Benjamin and Lucy Rowland Fund, Courtesy Museum of Fine Arts, Boston, 59

The Bettmann Archive, 28 (top), 30, 31, 35, 37, 38 (both), 42, 79, 82 (bottom), 88, 91

The British Museum, 46, 72

Catharine Page Perkins Fund, Courtesy Museum of Fine Arts, Boston, 15

Centennial Gift of Mr. and Mrs. Charles P. Lipson, Courtesy Museum of Fine Arts, Boston, 73 (bottom)

Classical Exchange Fund, Courtesy Museum of Fine Arts, Boston, 56

Corbis-Bettmann, 18, 33, 52 (bottom), 66, 68, 82 (top), 94

Courtesy, Museum of Fine Arts, Boston, 45, 84

Culver Pictures, Inc., 21

Edward J. and Mary S. Holmes Fund, Courtesy Museum of Fine Arts, Boston, 58

Gift of the Class of the Museum of Fine Arts, Mrs. Arthur L. Devens, Chairman, Courtesy Museum of Fine Arts, Boston, 45

Gift of Dr. and Mrs. Freddy Homburger, Courtesy Museum of Fine Arts, Boston, 8

Gift of E. P. Warren, Courtesy Museum of Fine Arts, Boston, 90

Gift of Mr. and Mrs. Benjamin Rowland, Courtesy Museum of Fine Arts, Boston, 89

Gift of Samuel and Edward Merrin; William Francis Warden Fund, Benjamin and Lucy Rowland Collection, by exchange, and Gift of Barbara Deering Danielson, by exchange, Courtesy Museum of Fine Arts, Boston, 57

H. L. Pierce Fund, Courtesy Museum of Fine Arts, Boston, 17, 28 (bottom), 69

Hulton Deutsch, 98

North Wind Pictures, 9, 11, 14, 20, 41, 43, 47 (bottom), 49, 50, 54, 60, 73 (top), 76, 81, 99

Ny Carlsberg Glyptotek, Copenhagen, 80

Original oil painting by Don Nardo, 47 (top)

Stock Montage, Inc., 24, 26, 27, 40, 52 (top), 61, 67, 70, 75, 78, 86, 97, 100

William Francis Warden Fund, Courtesy Museum of Fine Arts, Boston, 10

About the Author

Don Nardo is an award-winning author whose more than seventy books cover a wide range of topics, including science, health, and the environment. His main field, however, is history. Among his modern historical studies are *Braving the New World, The Mexican-American War, The U.S. Presidency,* and biographies of Thomas Jefferson, Franklin D. Roosevelt, and William Lloyd Garrison. Mr. Nardo's specialty is the ancient world, especially classical Greece and Rome, about which, in addition to this volume about life in Rome, he has written *The Battle of Marathon, The Age of Pericles, The Age of Augustus, Life in Ancient Greece, Cleopatra, The Battle of Zama, The Punic Wars,* and many others. Mr. Nardo also dabbles periodically in orchestral composition, oil painting, screenwriting, and film directing. He lives with his wife, Christine, on Cape Cod, Massachusetts.